MW01277337

I Love You, But ...

Brother Bob

Bloomington, IN

Milton Keynes, UK

AuthorHouse™
1663 Liberty Drive, Suite 200
Bloomington, IN 47403
www.authorhouse.com
Phone: 1-800-839-8640

AuthorHouse™ UK Ltd.
500 Avebury Boulevard
Central Milton Keynes, MK9 2BE
www.authorhouse.co.uk
Phone: 08001974150

This book is a work of non-fiction. Unless otherwise noted, the author and the publisher make no explicit guarantees as to the accuracy of the information contained in this book and in some cases, names of people and places have been altered to protect their privacy.

First published by AuthorHouse 4/7/2006

ISBN: 1-4259-0767-9 (sc)
ISBN: 1-4259-1252-4 (dj)

Printed in the United States of America
Bloomington, Indiana

This book is printed on acid-free paper.

I dedicate this book to my family, my friends and all of God's children. With out the Lord blessing me with you on my path, these letters could never have been written. Thank you for your love, your kindness, and for your prayers.

"I love you, but I could never love you as much as He does".

Brother Bob

Contents

Please Read, Before You Lay This Book Down

Aloha, Family, friends, brothers and sisters, and all of God's children,

When I first started to write these letters, it was not my plan to have them published. However, our plans are never the same as His plans. He has told me to send these letters out to His children. Being as humble as possible, I could not foresee such a task as this. I also would not have written it the way He has, nor had the wisdom to do so.

Through the Holy Spirit, I felt the desire to tell you how God has changed me. I wanted to share with you how hurt and sad I was growing up. I wanted to share with you how I feel from the heart, about the sorrow of everyday life from the eyes of an alcoholic.

I wrote these letters with the hope of sharing them one day with a few homeless men I know. However, anyone can gain something from reading them I believe.

Mr. Jerry Coffee, an ex-POW of Vietnam for six years, told me upon reading the first half of my book that if I were to have less self-pity and exchange that with lessons learned, that he believed that the book would be a huge success. I was blessed to hear such honest, warm, and thoughtful words of encouragement. Nevertheless, I feel that if I were to change what was in my heart at the time of each writing, I would lose what I felt in that moment. In other words, if I did not change things, you would be able to see the growing of my maturity in the Lord.

I also felt that the Lord did want me to reflect back to those days. I am aware of what it says in the Bible, "Brothers and Sisters, I do not consider myself yet to have taken hold of it. But one thing I do is forget what is behind and strain toward what is ahead. I press on toward the goal: to win the prize for which God has called me heavenward, in Christ Jesus. Each of us, who are mature, should take such a view of things. In addition, on some point you think differently, that, too, God will make clear to you. Only let us live up to what we have already attained" (Philippians 3:13-16).

This is what I hope I have done in these letters. I look at the past because I feel the Lord wanted me to share it with you. However, He also wants me to show you what it is that I have attained since those past years. At the end of this book, you will hear again from my heart, what wisdom I feel I have gained and how important that we as children of God must always remember: to love Him and one another before all things. It is because of my love for Him and you that I write these things. The Holy Spirit guides us. I believe in my heart as well that as it is written: "No one has seen, no ear has heard, no mind has conceived what God has prepared for those who love him…but God has revealed it to us by his Spirit" (1 Corinthians 2:9-10).

You see, I have found that you cannot truly Love God with out loving man. If anyone says "I love God," yet he hates his brother, he is as a liar. For anyone who does not love his brother, whom he has seen, cannot love God, whom he has not seen. In addition, he has given us this command: "Whoever loves God must also love his brother" (1 John 4:20-21).

My prayer is this, that you do not stop here and lay this book down because you think it is just another Christian book. I know in my heart that if you continue to read you will find yourself somewhere in it. You will read somewhere the answer to at least one of your questions. Trust in me my brother and sister, I am only giving you a small view of my life and hoping for the most. The most being that you find answers. I gain nothing; you gain wisdom. Why not take a chance for a change and seek wisdom over anything else?

I love you, but I could never love you as much as He does.

Brother Bob

A Pot of Gold at the End of the Rainbow

Aloha, friends and family, and all of God's children,

In the song, "Somewhere over the Rainbow," Judy Garland comes to the part where she says, "Why, oh why, can't I," meaning why oh why can't she have what is over that rainbow.

People feel that way. On the other hand, they may be searching for that pot of gold at the end of the rainbow. Meaning if a person "hit the jackpot" everything would be going his or her way for the rest of his or her life. It does not happen that way, so they become depressed and get drunk.

Have you ever thought about why you are not happy? Sure, you have. Everyone seems to be unhappy at certain times in his or her life. However, have you ever looked at yourself and said, "I have to face it; nothing's going to make me happy on this stupid earth with all the crap that's going on". Should your needs be met, you are still unhappy. So people say behind your back, "Look at that: she has all she could ever want or need and she's still unhappy. What an ungrateful person."

With me, I wanted to make people happy all of my life. That is because when I was six years old, I saw two older kids get into a fight. One was just getting the tar beat out of him. I tried to stop it even though I was only six. The one who was winning the fight pushed me away. I asked some of the older kids to stop it because I felt so sorry for the guy with blood all over him. No one would listen to me. When I went into the classroom, my legs were shaking like crazy. I could hardly walk; I was that weak. The teacher must have noticed something wrong with me because she asked me what was wrong. I was too scared to answer. (This teacher hated us Dunham boys. My older brothers caused her a lot of grief in the past, but I did not know this until later.) So, another boy answered the question for me by telling the teacher I had just saw someone get beat up in a fight.

The teacher then told me to "just get over it and pay attention to class." I was so scared that I had to go to the bathroom. This was the first day of school and I had just met the teacher from hell. In addition, I was so scared that I was afraid to ask if I could use the bathroom. Therefore, it happened: I wet my pants. As the other children begin to see the floor get wet, they started to giggle. The teacher asked what was so funny, and one of the kids said, "Bobby went to the bathroom on the floor."

She said, "You're just as bad as your brothers. Get over there, get some paper towels, and wipe that up. Then, when you're finished, I want you to go home and tell your parents what you did." I was crying and she said, "Stop that crying, too. I do not feel sorry for you and neither do the others. Get that wiped up and get straight home."

It was about twenty-two degrees outside that day, as I recall. There was about three or four inches of snow and I was freezing. We were poor children, being from a family of twelve children, and I had no gloves or warm clothes on. My pants were soaked from my mishap, and as I walked, they begin to freeze up. By the time I reached the front door of my home, my pants had frozen all the way through. I had to walk down the street looking like Frankenstein with his arms folded.

I was crying so hard because of the frozen pants rubbing against my legs, the embarrassment in school, and sadness of that boy getting beat up so badly, that when mother opened the door to see me, she must have been shocked. (I kicked on the door because my hands were too cold to open it.) I do not know if she ever did anything about that with the school. If she did, I did not hear about it, and when I asked my mother about it, forty-five years later, she said she did not remember it happening. Here I was, coming home from the first day of school and I had all of this happen to me.

As I look back, I can see how I started to turn into a bad boy. I seemed to be fighting with someone quite often. I am not a doctor but I believe that, at that time, I saw that no one was going to help me if anything happened to me or to others. I became an angry little man. I became the best rock thrower in town. I started a gang when I was twelve. (In the town of Mayberry — a.k.a. New Rockford — they thought so, anyway.) I was quite surprised when the police and the principal came into our class and took me and two other boys out of the room. When we got to the principal's office, my kid brother and two other boys were there as well. They said that I had to break up my gang. (Shoot, I didn't even know I had one.) Looking back, I can see how they thought I did.

My "friends" and I would go after the biggest kid in school on the playground and attack him. I remember all of us running up to this big kid, who was about six feet tall. We were only about four feet tall or less, and we would start to hit him in the legs and in the back. As the others were doing that, I would get a running start and fly into the air until I landed on his back. Then I would start to pull his hair and grab his nose and squeeze it. The others would be laughing hysterically as this big guy tried to fling me off. I would yell and say, "You think you're tough, don't you, you big s---."

It all seems funny now, but at that time, I really did dislike bigger kids. I guess it was my way of getting revenge for the person I saw getting beat up by the big boy in the churchyard that first day of school. "It was your fault that I wet my pants and nearly froze to death," I may have thought.

Of course, I truly believe that this all came about because I had no mentor in my life. My father (being the alcoholic that he was), certainly didn't have the time for me and my troubles. My mother was too busy taking care of my father and twelve children, so I grew up on my own; as did the rest of the children in my family. You could ask me this question: "Bob, do you feel like you want to get over the rainbow?" On the other hand, someone might ask, "Bob, are you searching for that pot of gold at the end of the rainbow?" I would reply to that with this:

When my older brother, George, went to be with the Lord, the pastor who spoke for us family members said, "Bob told me that his brother, your brother, had a rainbow over his heart." The pastor was right: I did say that. However, what I didn't tell the pastor is that George was also searching for that pot of gold at the end of the rainbow. As I was sitting there listening to the pastor, my mind went back to the time I had said something to George that he said he would always remember. That was this: "George, if you have to search for the pot of gold at the end of the rainbow, you have no pot of gold within your heart."

George knew what I meant when I said that. You see, George was a born-again Christian and he knew that if he kept that rainbow over his heart, loved everyone, and kept Jesus in his heart, that was his pot of gold. Jesus will always be the pot of gold with in the heart. The rainbow will always be overhead as long as we keep Jesus in our heart.

Have I found my pot of gold? You bet. Have I made it over the rainbow? You bet. Am I happy today? You bet. How could anyone ask for anything more?

"I love you, but I could never love you as much as He does."

Brother Bob

Please Listen

9/28/03

Aloha family, friends, and all of God's children,

Generation after generation has gazed upon the big screen to please the eye of whatever myth or fable appeared to the imagination. What has happened to our readers and poets? Where have the dreams of hope and desire gone? Why did the people sit back and say to the world, "I'm tired of trying to help and tired of learning just to get nowhere in this lost existence."

People in general appear to be stable in their life. However, so many judge others by the kind of job they have and how pretty their wife or husband may be. If our neighbor has a home that is livable for any movie star, then we smile because we have one just as good next door. We are proud to be as rich as the "guy next door."

I have heard many times, "Life is filled with surprises, so you better be ready for the worst." Does being ready for the worst mean that you have to seek to have more and live better than others in order to fulfill your happiness? What can I do if I cannot live up to society's expectations? "I know; I'll fight this joke of a society and go out in the streets and find a new and better way to live. I will make a difference somehow by helping those who are less fortunate than I am (according to my so-called intelligence). There must be a way to bring the good out of everyone. There has to be a dream in everyone's eye, just as those who watch it on the big screen, whom I can reach. I can make a difference if I seek to endure the hardship of such a lifestyle."

Therefore, I set out to do just that: make a difference. "We learn by our mistakes." Who said that? It must have been the same person who said, "Everything is by trial and error." Making a difference wasn't planned, at least not in the openness of my mind, but maybe in the back corner of it. What happened to me was more than "trial and error." What happened was what I created to happen. I could blame no one for the pain and sorrow I suffered. I had no one to complain to for my sleepless nights and my broken bones. No one said, "I have to go to the streets and be with out." So where did it get me? These are little stories upon refection of days and years past. It is not what I got out of life, (it's not over yet) but what I am getting out of life. I don't dwell on the past but I do reflect at times.

Dan was a man who had more anger about life than most men I have met. He was hard to get to know. He said few words and never looked happy. When I was introduced to Dan, he was stoned on coke, ice, H, or whatever drug was available for the day. I liked him, however, because I could see knowledge in his eyes and that made me curious to know more. He must have seen something he liked about me, as well, because he started to share his story almost immediately with me. Dan was a Vietnam veteran (our connection) who was addicted on drugs and lost everything that was important to him. His wife left him and he was "barred" from his family ties. (Another black sheep.) He spoke of the anger in the world when he came home from "the Nam" and the sadness of the people around him daily. "Drugs are not an option, they are a way out." He said to me one day. "A way out of what, brother?" I asked. "Out of… trying to figure out what is wrong with this world", He answered.

I listened to Dan's story for a couple of hours and then he asked me what I was doing on the streets. As I began to tell him what and why I felt the way I did about life, Dan began to drift away. He would glance over at me from time to time, but he obviously was not interested in what I had to say. I found that 85 percent of the people I spoke to did not listen. Whoever's path I crossed told me their story but would drift off when I began to tell mine. "Everyone wants to speak but no one wants to listen," just like in "the world," I thought to myself. Therefore, I learned my first lesson: "If you're going to be out on the streets, Bob, listen and hear, observe, and be understanding."

(Have you ever thought about that? Do you listen and observe? Are you compassionate to others, or do you want to be heard only?)

Kathy was always smiling. She has a way of making you believe that what you said was important. This was a surprise to me. Kathy actually cared. That's what I thought when I first met her. She was running with another homeless man, Jack. Jack was a 'Nam vet', as well. I found out that Kathy was a hustler. She would use any man to get what she wanted. I didn't care. I would be doing the same to her; what goes around comes around.

I had become pretty good at deception and became somewhat of a grifter. I called myself a grifter, not a drifter. (A grifter is a con man. I never heard of that word, "grifter," until years later, but I like it better than "con man." Even though grifter "sounds" better, it still means that you are a disgusting person in our society and with in the court system.) Kathy told me that she was from New Orleans. She said she was in jail there and when she got out, she came to Southern California. (I had been in California for about four months.) I asked her what she was in jail for and she said, "I stabbed my boyfriend in the chest with a kitchen knife." (I mentally formed a picture of me sleeping with her; suddenly, she decides to stab me in the middle of the night with a plastic fork out of the garbage can.) This stabbing happened late at night, she said. The police took her to jail and told her on the way that her boyfriend was pronounced dead at the scene. Kathy was going to go to prison for murder, or worse, get the death penalty. In the morning after, one of her cellmates came to her and said, "You lucky bitch, the son of a bitch lived."

Kathy and I went through a lot on the street together. We where known in the Riverside County area as the best panhandlers around. We made a good team so we supplied booze for all those around our group of "good people." If we knew someone was bad news when approaching us in the park, we would defend one another to the end. If someone in our group got out of line, they would have to move on. Such was the story with "Jack." Jack and Kathy used to be a team. When I showed up, they had parted ways. The way it came about was like this: I walked up to a table near the area that had about seven people sitting around. I played it like I was just passing through, and I knew better than to have eye contact. (Never have eye contact with street people; they get very nervous.) However, I would look at the situation out of the corner of my eye and I saw Kathy paying close attention to me.

Therefore, I played as if I was just a "lost child." She either fell for it, or picked up on my play, but either way, we knew we would hook up. We did after everyone was drunk. I became friends with them fast. The two 'Nam vets liked me and told me to stay around awhile. I liked Jack at first. We became friendly. The problem with Jack was that he only wanted to fight when he knew his opponent was too drunk to defend himself. He also knew that I would fight anyone but my 'Nam brothers. I felt it was wrong to hurt someone who was already hurting as bad as I was, inside. Hurting people hurt people. After that little drunk, Kathy and I ended up with one another that night.

I figured there would always be some pain with in Jack because I was with Kathy. Therefore, I asked Kathy if she would like to go to Seattle for a short time. Time to get away from the boredom, and she agreed. When Kathy and I left for Seattle, she looked bad. Even though she was quite pretty and had a great little body, she had bad teeth and a crow's nest for hair. Therefore, when we were in Seattle, I arranged for her to have her teeth fixed and her hair styled. What a huge difference that made. As they would say in my day, she was a "knockout." I would like to tell you more about that trip but that is another story.

After three months in Seattle, we wanted to head out of town . Therefore, I stole a car from someone in a bar. The guy said he knew me from school, so I asked him if I could borrow his car to show Kathy around town. I had already told him we were homeless and we were living in an abandoned van. He trusted me, but his two friends did not. Therefore, his two friends followed us until I lost them on some side street. Then, I asked Kathy if she wanted to go back to California. Of course, I knew she would agree because it was getting cold in Seattle.

When we arrived back in the park, we hung out at in Riverside County where we were happy to see everyone. Many of them didn't even recognize Kathy with her new look. Some were shocked, including Jack. We all drank our wine and before long, I was passed out. When I awoke in the morning, Kathy was sitting on the bench, looking at me. I knew something had happened while I slept. I asked what was wrong and she said I better go and look in a mirror somewhere. So we went to another park and when I looked in the mirror, I saw knife cuts on my neck and a split lip with dried blood.

I said, "It looks like someone cut my throat after they split my lip. Why didn't they kill me? What changed their minds?" Then I thought to myself that Kathy must have said something to someone about what we did in Seattle. Jack came to mind.

Kathy said, "Jack did it while you were passed out."

I said, "Why did he stop?"

"Big Dave stopped him," she said, "Jack hit you while you where lying on the ground, and then went to get the knife you gave him. He came back and started to cut you one slice at a time. Dave stepped in and picked Jack up like a bag of potatoes. Dave told him to fight you when you're sober, not passed out."

The knife that I gave Jack was his to begin with. One day, Jack came to me and asked me if I wanted a knife he had. I asked to see it and I was surprised with what I saw. It was a brass knuckled eight-inch blade knife with gold on most of it. It was very nice. It was very well grafted, but frightful to look at just as well. I said, "I use my hands and feet in a fight, Jack; I don't need this." I was afraid of what I would do with it, really. I asked him why he didn't want it and he said he was afraid he would kill someone with it. (Surprise). When Kathy and I had set out for Seattle, I gave it back to him before we left. This was a big mistake.

I said to Kathy, "You told him what happened between you, me, and Jessie in Seattle, didn't you? (We had a threesome and Jessie is black, which would really anger Jack.) She said yes. After telling her that she had made a big mistake, I told her she would be responsible for Jack's death, not me. I had no choice; I had to take Jack out. If I didn't, Jack would be cutting much deeper the next time he found me passed out.

We went back to the park and we sat with the group. Everyone played the game of letting things happen the way they thought it would. After looking around, I saw Jack walking up to the table. Everyone looked at me with anticipation; sure of what was to come. (I was not going to do what everyone expected.)When Jack reached the table, I told him that we needed to talk in private. We walked about fifty yards away, out of ear shot, and I said to him, "Brother Jack, I've been good to you. You know I have always said that I wouldn't fight a 'Nam brother. Now you've gone over the line. I'm taking Kathy with me to another place. I'm not going to drink for two weeks, and then Kathy and I are coming back here. Jack, when I come back, one of us is going to die. There isn't room in this park for the two of us any longer. Do you understand me, Jack? One of us is going to die and I have no plans to leave anytime soon." Jack kept looking down when I spoke to him. When I finished talking, he just nodded his head and we started to walk back to the bench. As we came closer to the bench, Jack said he had to go somewhere and he would talk to us later. No one saw him again; at least I didn't. Kathy and I left and then came back in two weeks as I told everyone we would. One in our group said Jack disappeared when we did. (Somehow, they heard about the conversion between Jack and me. (They may have thought that I killed him already.)

Kathy ended up back in New Orleans and the last I heard, about a year ago, Jack got a fin (five years in prison) shortly after we saw him in the park. No one has seen or heard from him since. Kathy ended up doing five in her state for drugs. I am also glad to hear that she found the Lord while in prison and is now just fine since getting out of prison. I am very happy for her, and I do miss her. I think of her often and of the things, we endured.

I loved every one of these people. They were good people. They had no money, they judged no one, and they were "for real." I forgave those who hurt me. I wish that I could see each one of them again. However, life does not wait for anyone...We just have to take it one day at a time. We have choices to make, but in the end, God has the last say. Maybe, one day I will see Kathy and Dave. I found out many of those people have died. However, as for those who survived, I cannot help but believe that somewhere along the path they chose, they answered the door. They opened that door when God knocked and they have found out what life is "really all about." God bless them all.

Before you turn on the TV the next time you sit down, think about someone you love and give him or her call instead. Write a letter or send them a postcard. You may think that someone you know does not love you as much as you would like him or her to. If you write a letter to them, you may be surprised of the kind of reply you get. Take time out to listen to others, near or far, next door or on the street, they will love you for it, and so will He.

I love you, but I could never love you as much as He does.

Brother Bob

He's More Than Everything

Aloha family, friends and all of God's children,

"You can't be!"

"That is impossible!"

"How stupid are you that you would believe that anything remotely like that is possible?"

People talk down to us at times. Have you ever sat down and tried to figure out what this world is really all about? Those who have really searched their hearts have found the answer. Most of them were lonely and/or depressed at the time. Others have had reason to look with in, to take a hard look at life, instead of running or simply ignoring what is missing. Do you really want to know what it's all about? If you do, I know the answer, and it is more than anything you could fathom or explain in words. It is everything. Let me rephrase that, it is not an "it" but a "He."

You see, until you find who "He" is, you have no real life here on earth, or a purpose. It is impossible to know "what it's all about" until "you" stop looking for the answers to life. You cannot find the answers, He teaches you what life is all about. "Once you ask Him for his help, you will find that He is everything." I hear that statement from Christians often. However, I have found that if you go beyond the "everything" you will find that He is "more than everything."

Many trying times come before us as we walk along His path. Many wonder why these trials and struggles come to what we think is "the limit." God never gives to us more than we can handle. He always has a reason for all that He does. We think to ourselves as we go through these struggles, "Why me, Lord?" Then He takes us onto another level of time, another path, where we say the same thing over again, Why me, Father? We do not have the answers to all the questions, but He does. We think we know everything about life. We don't; we just fool ourselves now and then. He not only knows everything, but also is more than everything we can know, say, or do.

Many times when I was homeless, others who lived on the streets came to me for comfort or compassion. I somehow would find in me a way to ease their pain. Often, I would help them ease that pain with a bottle of wine or a shot of vodka. However, there were many times, also, when I would tell them that they should go to a church for help or talk to a minister. I could give them that advice (and few took it) but I myself wouldn't think of doing it. I was going to find the answers myself. I didn't need anyone's help. I was going to figure out this whole messed-up problem in the world by myself. However, one day, someone set fire to our camp just on the outskirts of town. At the time, I had a full-length cast on my right leg (given to me out of the kindness by an off-duty police officer). As we got closer to camp we saw flames and fire trucks. Kathy ran ahead of me to see what had happened. She quickly ran back toward me. She had been running so fast that when she had come upon me, she could not slow down. She and I hit the ground with good force.

I asked, "What the heck happened?"

Kathy said, "Someone started the fire on purpose. Whoever it was didn't know that Doc was passed out in the grass."

I asked, "How bad is he?"

She said, "As far as the policeman and medics could tell, the right side of his face is burned and he had lost his right ear, at the minimum."

I didn't see Doc for some time after that. Then, one day, he came walking up to us in the park, and I could not believe it was him. He had a suit on and he looked like one of the clerks in the unemployment center. (That is what I imagined to myself, anyway; I had not been to work long enough to collect unemployment.) Doc came up to me and gave me a huge hug. I asked him where he had been besides the hospital, and he told me the following story.

"It was something, Bob," he said, "I came awake in the ambulance on the way to the hospital. I had no idea what had happened. All I remember is hearing voices, and the next thing I knew, I was on my way to the hospital. I didn't feel any pain because of the booze but I sure felt it in the hospital. When they finally let me have visitors, my father and mother came in to see me. I was shocked because my father is a real hard-nosed case and he said he wanted nothing to do with me last time I saw him." As Doc told his story, tears began to well in his eyes. He spoke of how his father and he had forgiven one another and how his mother cried to see her family together again. I could see that the whole situation had been very traumatic for him, and yet joyful. Somehow, I knew there had to be more for him to have changed so drastically. Drastic isn't the word here… "different" is more like it.

I asked him, "What made such a big change in your life? I didn't think that you were the kind of man who would change his life around because of a few tears and a couple of hugs." If you knew Doc like I did, you would know that he did things his way and his way only. Doc had a heart of gold; he also was very stubborn and committed to doing things his way. He said, "Bob, I know you're a lot like me. We see things the way they are and we take no prisoners." (Doc was a Vietnam vet, one of the things that we had in common.) "But you're missing something, Bob, that I thought was never in existence." He then told me about how his sister came to the hospital and she told him about how God wanted to help him and to save him from any more pain. Doc told me that he and his sister prayed that day and he gave his life to the Lord. Doc then told me something I will always remember. Doc said, "Bob, if you really want to find any peace on this ^#+% earth, you're going to have ask God for His help or die." I knew Doc was speaking from the heart, even if he said it so blatantly.

I did not see Doc again. I was told he was staying with his folks until he was healthy enough to go out in "the world." Many times over the years, I thought about what he told me. It wasn't until six years later, (from a person I kept in touch with on the streets) that I heard he had died. I wasn't told how he died, but I was sure of one thing: he died knowing he was going to a better place. That is all Doc wanted in life: to have a better place to lay his head. He saw too much sorrow and sadness. When we had that last conversation, I knew in my heart that he had found something on earth that I wanted. I just did not want it as bad as he did at that time in my life. Doc had shown me by the expression in his eyes that God was "more than everything" he had ever imagined.

Do you really want to know what He is about? Do you want to know that He is "more than everything" you imagined? Then all you have to do is open the door when He knocks.

Please keep your door open to be filled with His love and His joy.

I love you, my brothers and sisters, but I can never love you as much as He does.

Brother Bob

How Come?

5/1/04

Aloha, my friends, family, and all of God's children,

Someone once told me to, "never start stories with a question". (I had to question that.) However, it brought to my mind a question that many will ask another every day. That is this: "Why did God do that if He's real?" I am not the only one on earth who knows the answer.

Listen: do you remember when you were young and your parents told you to do something you did not want to do? Sure you do! No matter how hard you would fight to get your way, you would not. As an adult, you came to realize that everything they did was for your betterment so that you would learn right from wrong. Our Father in heaven is no different than your father here on earth was when you were growing up. Once you know that Jesus died for you, and you ask God for forgiveness of your sins, you start life in an adult body, but as a child learning new things. However, I cannot teach you how to do what He wants, nor can anyone else. That is why God sent the Holy Spirit, to help us along the way. (You learn by His guidance through the Holy Spirit.) It's quite simple to understand, but we (I know I did) make it hard on ourselves because we think we know it all.

I do not want to scare you off with what I believe it takes or how I think you should go about learning what God is all about. However, I would like to tell you a story about how I learned firsthand how He guides me and why I do not ask, "Why did God do that if He's real?"

When I left Tripler Hospital, in February of 1995, I had no desire to touch a glass of liquor again or to have a beer with the boys. I "knew," by way of the Holy Spirit, that I would never be the way I was: An Alcoholic. That was the first time I knew God had control of my life. I didn't ask Him why. I didn't have to be a genius to know that if I kept on drinking, I would die soon.

I then moved to the Big Island, Hawaii, to help one of my brothers who lived there. After I had been there for three weeks, God told me to go to Kailua-Kona, which was about an hour away. "I didn't ask Him why." I knew I was supposed to by way of the Holy Spirit.

Next, He told me I would have to live in a halfway house (a place for alcoholics and drug addicts). This time I did ask, I said, "God, why do I have to go here when I already know that you took away the desire for alcohol?" I didn't hear anything. This ticked me off. I could have said, "That's it, if you're real, you wouldn't have me go here." However, because I trusted Him to take away the alcohol in the first place (and He did), I knew that even though I did not hear an answer, I knew by way of the Holy Spirit that I must do this. "I had to listen to Dad, just as I did when I was a lad."

After I had spent three months at the halfway house, I went to stay with a couple of women whom I had come to know. About a week or so after, I asked our Father what it was that He wanted me to do next. I said, "Where's my sheep? Where is the flock I'm to take care of?" Well, I was not prepared for the shock that was to come. If ever I had any doubt before, this sure cleared that up. I say this because the next day, I looked into the help wanted adds and there in the maintenance section was an ad for a caretaker. I was quite sure I could get this job, but just in case, I prayed about it. I said, "Father, if this is where you want me to work and to have a place to study your word [the Bible], then you will have to make it very clear to me. And if it is, I want to thank you now for your help and guidance."

I went to see a friend of mine who helped get me stable in Kailua-Kona when I first arrived. We had become very close friends and she would later be instrumental, as a board member, for the success of my non-profit company.

After I told her that there was a place up in the mountain area that needed a landscaper and maintenance man, she asked me what the address was. After I had told her, she said, "I can't believe it. That place belongs to my best friend. We grew up together and partied together before we both became sober. We went to school together, Bob. Oh Bob, you have this job. I'll call her and tell her you're coming."

I should tell you a few things that were said in this add in the paper. I already told you that they wanted a landscaper and maintenance man, but it also said that a two-story house comes with it. That house would be rent-free of course; that was part of the deal. However, there would be no salary. I would have to get a part-time job somewhere else. (I had no problem with that because I could do house painting. I had been a painter for fifteen years.)

Therefore, I went to my interview the next day. When I arrived, I was greeted by two very nice people around my age, in their forties. After sitting and talking about my experience, the owner said he had six and a half acres of land. He asked me, "Would you like to take a look, since you have the job?" I was excited to hear those words, to say the least. As we started down the driveway he pointed toward a two-story house and said that I would be living in it. It used to be a barn and they had fixed it up to look like the barn you would see on the old TV show, Mr. Ed. (Really.) It was a great-looking house. It had the fold-out little shutters on the windows and everything else that pertained to that show on TV. As we walked a little further, a flock of sheep came running toward us to greet Don, the owner. I could not believe it. Here was my flock of sheep I had asked our Father for and I had to laugh. I was so excited. I had those little happy vibes going up and down my back and happiness in my stomach. I never looked at God as having a sense of humor before. This had to be one of His classics. When Don asked me why I was laughing, I told Him what God had just showed me and he started to laugh as well. (Don is also a Christian.)

I stayed at the home for over a year. Did I ask God why I had to live there? No, but I knew there was a reason other than taking care of the sheep. I later found out there was. It was while I was there that God told me to start my non-profit company, and to learn more about Him and Jesus. It was there that I grew stronger, not only physically, but mentally as well. I regained my self-confidence, my integrity, and my faith grew stronger.. I had come to this place not knowing what, where, how, or why I was even on the Big Island. However, I knew that I was given favor by God.

So when someone should ask me, "If there really is a God, why did this happen?" I say, "Once I came to have a personal relationship with the Lord, I no longer had to ask that question. For if you truly love His Son, and Him as well, you will know better then to ask why. You will just say, "Thank You, Father, for all of your wisdom and guidance."

Do I know the answers to the question of, "How Come…?" No, but then, I don't need to.

I love you, but I could never love you as much as He does.

Brother Bob

Your Ticket Home

Aloha family, friends, and all of God's children,

One of the many things we all go through in life is fighting ourselves. I would use so many emotions and try to think through every decision as if my life depended on it. Have you ever thought to yourself, "I have to figure this out and I'm not going to be satisfied until I do?" I used to do that all the time. I always seemed to think the worst of everything. Yet, I always seemed to find a way out. All of that thinking and or worrying for naught.

After many years of this one-sided battling, I taught myself to just listen and observe instead of being opinionated and argumentative. It was the easy way out. It was what I felt was a wise way out of conflict and resolution. I would stand in the shadows of time. I have since come to see that only God has the right answer in what we should or should not do. Certainly, we have our common sense and our gut feelings. Nevertheless, when it comes down to a solution to a tough decision it would be wise, and a relief as well, to have no doubt as to whether you are right or wrong about your choices? "How is that possible to begin with?" Thank you for asking. I will tell you.

I was watching Pastor Charles Stanley on the TV yesterday morning and he was on the topic of success. I have read his book, How to Succeed God's Way, but I still wanted to hear what he had to say on the subject. Charles told of seven things you cannot do if you want to be successful in doing things God's way and not your own. Those seven things included fear, doubt, excuses, procrastination, greed, violation of our conscience, and slothfulness.

These seven steps are not your ticket home, but they are a good start on your way to the airport. Getting started is the first step to success. "Nevertheless, what are you leading to here, Brother Bob?" Well shoot,

I'm glad you asked. I want to tell you a story. Yesterday, I went to a meeting to help support Mr. Jerry Coffee in his campaign for a seat in the House of Representatives here on Oahu (State House District 33). You have read in previous letters about us e-mailing one another.

This was the first time we would meet since those e-mails. I found Him to be very honest and he has a wonderful family. He introduced me to our governor, Linda Lingle and others at the meeting as we waited for him to speak. Once I found my seat, I went over the pamphlets and an introductory letter of his goals and ambitions to help us out here on Oahu.

As I mentioned before, Brother Jerry is a Vietnam veteran. However, what I did not tell you is that he also received the Silver Star, Legion of Merit, Distinguished Flying Cross, Bronze Star, and Purple Heart while in the service of our country. In addition, did I mention that he was in a Vietnam prison camp for six years as well? I learned much more about this child of God and I am very pleased to be a part of helping him in his election. One of the things that hit home with me is the fact that he wants to help stop the drug problem we have here. We have the highest population of alcoholics, drug users, and homeless per capita in the U.S.A. I have no idea if Jerry knows this. (I found out this news while doing my outreach program on the Big Island.)

Jerry wants to have more treatment centers and he told me that maybe he could use my help in that area. I feel so blessed by this opportunity. It was in my heart by the Lord to help these people long ago and maybe now I could help in a big way. Thank you, Lord. However, one of the things that happened to Jerry in Vietnam hit my heart: this is the story he told. Jerry said, "When I first arrived at the prison camp, they put us in these separate hooch's. As I walked into the one I was to stay in, I noticed something written on one of the beams. These words are what sustained me during those years. There were just two words. The first word was God, and then there was an equal sign and then the word Strength: God = Strength".

God = Strength. How true that is. Brother Jerry didn't succeed by his strength alone. He succeeded by the strength with in him by the grace of God. Many of you who are reading this story may feel that you can make it on your own, or, have made it on your own up to this day. That is fine and dandy. However, have you ever thought to yourself, "What if God gave me the strength to go on"?

I have told you from the beginning of these letters that I am not trying to convince you in any way about who God and Jesus are. Nevertheless, I think you will find that if you took the time to read the Bible and get answers to your questions, you would not be as confused about life. Open up your mind. Don't do as I did for all of those years and stand in the shadows of doubt and confusion. We may think we have a lot of time, but we really do not. If you are in your teens or in your twenties right now, I want to tell you something, I wish I had learned when I was your age: "I'm not as smart as I think I am."

There is no one on the earth who knows everything, so what makes you think you know more than God does? Find out if I speak the truth by asking God yourself if you are "all that." Trust me: you are not all that. However, you can be all that God wants you to be just by asking Him.

Do you think you are going to get that ticket home when the time has come to take flight? I know I am. You can, too. Do as Brother Jerry did after his plane went down. As you are starting to get back on your feet, keep your eyes focused upward. You will be flying home on a oneway ticket to paradise if you keep this thought in your mind: God = Strength.

I love you, but I could never love you as much as He does.

Brother Bob

Life's Creation

Aloha family, friends, and all of God's children,

Norman Vincent Peale, a Protestant pastor, wrote The Power of Positive Thinking. He once said the following when asked what he believes is the meaning of life: "We are here to be excited, youth to old age, to have an insatiable curiosity about the world." Aldous Huxley once said that to carry the spirit of the child into old age is the secret of genius. Moreover, I buy that. We are here to genuinely, humbly, and sincerely help others by practicing a friendly attitude. Moreover, every person is born for a purpose. Everyone has a God-given potential, in essence, built into them. If we are to live life to its fullest, we must realize that potential.

We are the children of God, one and all. If your choice is to live this life as a person set to see things your way only, please listen. Take the time, the most important few minutes of your life, to hear what God has to say about why you are here. Do this by doing one simple thing: asking Him. You know that in your heart we are not here to be alone, to be doing things not as we see them, but as He sees them. Everyone knows this in his or her heart.

As Pastor Peale so clearly stated, "Everyone has a God-given potential, in essence, built into them." Ask Him what it is; you will always be grateful for what you will hear.

I love you, but I could never love you as much as He does.

Brother Bob

Visual Mind

Aloha, family, friends and all of God's Children,

From what you have read thus far in my letters, you must surely know that I am very honest and say what I know to be the truth in all matters concerning my past and present. Therefore, I pray that this next story will not sway your mind to thoughts of anything other than the truth as you know me to write. For what I will tell you now is just as truthful as what you have read in past words.

I have a vision. Martin Luther King had a vision. You and many others as well have visions. However, have you ever experienced a visual mind?

"What's that?" you say. It is the ability to see what God wants you to see, in your mind. Let me try to explain this to you. When you walk down the street with your eyes closed, you see in your mind what the sidewalk looks like. On the other hand, if you are sitting down with your eyes closed and a friend puts something strange in your hand, you visually try to see what it is by touch and feel. These are mind visions.

When God gives you a vision of His mind; it is about the future and the past that you did not see before through your eyes, or your mind's eye, as it were.

These are different types of visions. What I want to try to explain is a vision that God has and He shows it to you, like when He spoke to me audibly. As He spoke to me, in my mind, I saw all that He said. He was showing me my past. Then He went on further and told me my future. He did not show me the exact place I would be, or the people I would meet. He showed me thousands and thousands of people in one large group and I was talking to them. He showed me different countryside's and land space throughout the world. It was His mind guiding mine, you could say. It was His vision being shown with in my mind. It was as if He had control of my mind but He did not let me feel as though He was taking over my mind. He was more or less sharing His thoughts with me. As He did this, He spoke to me. It was audible, just as if there were a stereo in my mind. He had full control of my mind. It was strange at first. It was overwhelming. I am sure it was just as overwhelming to Paul or Moses and all others that have heard His voice. There are thousands of people whom God has talked to audibly. These people are afraid to tell family or friends of their experience because they are afraid of what people will think of them. Fear of being called crazy, etc., etc. When I told three of my brothers while riding in a car with them, they listened very intently. Not one of them said I was crazy because they know me to be honest. Nevertheless, I could see their doubts. If the shoe where on the other foot, and even if I did have a personal relationship with Jesus, I would have reacted as they did. I would have listened, I would have thought that what I was hearing was being said in honesty, but I would have had doubts. Why? Because people in general tend not to understand things that they cannot feel, touch, smell, hear or see. I would not try to convince you of what happened. There are even those who are ministers who have doubt that what I say is true.

Listen: this does not mean I am special, quite the contrary, actually. In God's eyes, each one of us is special to Him. That is what is beautiful about walking His path: we know we are loved but we are humble about it. We want to go out and tell the world about this new life, but alas, people cannot accept it unless they experience it for themselves. Again, I am not preaching. I am just telling you what happened. I know one minister who told me he was jealous because God spoke to me and not himself. He wasn't jealous in the sense of the word, but more envious, I would say. He told me this in a loving and honest way. That kind of reaction is what I would expect. I would have been feeling the same way if someone new in the Lord came up to me and told me God spoke to him. What if I had been walking the Lord's path for twenty years and He never said, "Hey, Brother Bob, what's cooking, dude?" Then He went to talk to this "new kid," and started telling him who was going to win the next lottery. (Just kidding, He wouldn't do that.) I would be a little miffed, at first. However, I would then think about it and know that God works in each of us in a different way. Because He spoke to me, does not mean He loves me more than He loves any other child of

His. It all depends on what He has planned for each of us and how He wants to get the message across to us. He has a vision for each of us. You just have to ask Him what it is He wants you to do. You will not know unless you ask. Maybe He is waiting for you to check out His sound system. (Over His sound system, there is a sign that says, "Can You Hear Me Now"? ;-)

I'm getting too deep. You will have to read the Bible and listen to a minister to learn all there is to learn about such matters. I pray that one day you may see and hear what I do. I will never, try to push anything down your throat. I know what that is like and it turned me off for years. I was "beaten with the Bible," by family members when I was growing up. That was not right. It is one's choice. I only pray you see things His way soon. Time is short and I love you too much to see you suffer with out Him. I have so much that I would like to say to you. Because you have no understanding of His ways, I would be wasting your time as well as my own. However, on the other hand...

I would like to quote scripture here:

> *Not that I speak in respect of want: for I have learned, in whatever state I am, therewith to be content.*
>
> (Philippians 4:11)

Contentment is not getting what we want, but being satisfied with what we have. Because I have Jesus in my life, I have been able to see everything as contentment. We all go through hard times. If you are living life with the Lord, however, "you know," that everything will be okay no matter what the outcome. Nevertheless, it is hard at times because you always want to do things your way instead of His. (This is called, living in the flesh, in the Bible.) Such is why we are ministered to and read in the Bible, that we must put on a suit of armor.

God's vision for you is all planned out. He knows what you are going to do before you do it. Isn't that something? Anyway, I am grateful to Him for sharing with me what He has planned. It gives me hope daily and helps me to endure those hard times that come around. His vision and everything else that He does is for us. How in the world could I be of want when I know that He will never let me down in the end? I cannot. That is something indeed.

When God told me that I would no longer drink booze, I knew it was so. I haven't had a drink in ten years. No matter what you believe a Christian should be, you must never forget that he is human and he will make mistakes. I could drink tomorrow if I wanted to. It would be my choice if I did so. What I am saying is that His word is good; it is we humans who mess things up. We can not go through life thinking that we are alone. If you do, you will be.

I love you, but I could never love you as much as He does.

Brother Bob

The Garden, God, and I

We go through life thinking that things have to be the way they are just "because that's the way it is." This is not true in most cases, and the one who knows this the most is God.

Let me explain: I used to believe that if someone told me something and I trusted this person, that, well, it must be so. In most cases, we all do that. We want to believe that what that person says is true, because if he or she is wrong, we look stupid for believing them in the first place. We don't want to look stupid, now, do we? Say that at one time someone told you a certain thing about another person that was a bad thing. You believed it to be true. Now you have this view of the "said person" as a bad person or someone you cannot trust. Now, right now you may be thinking to yourself, "Well, that's just gossip." No, it is more than that. Many people who were good people, go bad because of someone else's hurtful words. When you say something about a person, and it isn't true, you cause the person that you lied about to have a life of sadness, pain, distrust of others, etc., until finally, complete destruction ensues.

I know: It happened to me. I had friends. (At least I thought they were friends.) When they heard lies about me, it hurt so bad that I wanted to kill someone. I ended up going into the Marines to kill somebody in Vietnam. I also wanted to see my older brothers who were in Vietnam at the time. However, the main reason was to get away from those who had hurt me. When I was discharged from the Marines, I found that things were not any different then when I went in. Only now, I saw more dishonesty and lies than ever before. People said things about me that could never have happened if I wanted them to. They begin to label me as a con artist, a thief, and a hustler. I did hustle on the pool table, and I did lie my way out of trouble. I, at times, talked my way into a job. However, I did not steal from my friends. I did not con my friends. I did not hustle my friends. In my mind, I was surviving in a world of dishonesty and corruption. The government was the bad guy, not me. Therefore, I stole some food and booze from the store. I took money from women and beat people on the pool table for money. I was going to beat them at their own game in life. I was not going to, "be pushed around," any longer. I was not going to be, fooled, again by a government that only lied to me and took away my friends and family members. My thinking was, "The government killed my older brother in a veteran's hospital and they do not deserve my respect, no more than the people who hurt me all my life". I was angry and I was hurt. That is what caused me to go to the streets.

Once in Seattle, I had to sleep in the snow. I had to sleep on cardboard, as well as covering up with it. I nearly froze to deaththat night because I was too proud to ask anyone for help. I thought if I was not going to ask for help, I might as well go to a place where the climate is warmer. I had that chance when a friend, a Vietnam brother, asked me if I wanted to go California with him and two other friends of ours. I jumped on the chance to go where it was warm.

That trip ended up with me going through all sorts of trials and tribulations. I tell of some of those times in some of my writings. What I had found out while I was in California is that I had a heart for the homeless. I soon found myself not only helping them to get food, but I was able to console them as well. I found that many of the homeless came to me because I had a positive attitude and I would find ways to get them jobs if they wished to work.

Years later, five of my brothers came down to California to "rescue" me from the street. I didn't think they where rescuing me at the time, but they were. I would have more than likely been dead if I had stayed. After all, I had my throat cut, had a gun pulled on me, and had my legs broken twice while I was there. I always had to watch my back.

Although I went to five treatment centers for alcohol and drugs, it still did not stop me from using. I thought if I moved to Hawaii, things would be different. Moreover, it was a new beginning, as far as drinking went. I met a wonderful woman (who I ended up marrying), and I became a born-again Christian. This will be hard for those of you reading this letter to believe, but God spoke to me audibly. However, you will never believe that if you do not know Christ as your personal savior. If you do not know God, you will never be able to understand much of anything that is important in His eyes.

Why am I telling you all of this? It is for the following reasons: I found a place where there is peace, joy, hope, and love; true love, "A Garden of Eden". It is a place where everything and everyone who I meet is good and has positive thoughts. It is not heaven, although I wish it were, but it is as close to heaven as you can get living here on earth. However, there is only one way to find it. You must ask God for forgiveness of your sins. As well, you must tell our Father how grateful you are for His only begotten Son's sacrifice. You must tell Him that you know with in your heart that Jesus truly did die for our sins and believe it with all of your heart and soul.

I never would have believed there was a God if I did not ask Him for His help. I wanted to help the young, the old, the elderly, and the homeless. He knew that once I said that I believed in His son and asked for forgiveness, that I was being truly honest with Him and myself. That is why He spoke to me and has continued to speak to me (but not audibly any longer, but thru the Holy Spirit) whenever I ask Him for His help. Praise God.

This garden is "Jesus in my heart." Whenever I want to be with Him, all I have to do is ask Him to be with me. Then, we will sit and talk for hours about life, about kindness, about helping others, and much, much more. It is so peaceful just being with Him. If ever I am sad, I know whom to call on. Just do not take my word for it; ask Him for yourself. You will find that "Garden of Peace," as well. I have told you many personal things about me. I told you them so that you could see the hate and the anger that I once had in me. I no longer suffer with in. I no longer worry about what people say or what tomorrow will bring. I live that "one day at a time" that they talked so much about in AA meetings. It is true: when you walk with God, the only thing that matters is if you are doing something to help others today. I can help all the people I have ever wanted to now. If they do not want my help, I pray that some day soon they will ask God for His.

I love you, but I could never love you as much as He does.

Brother Bob

Dear Pastor Tompkins

October 3, 1995

As I was walking home along the beach here in Kona, Hawaii, I was praying for direction in my life. I was on my way to the Veterans' Administration office to talk to my counselor. My intuition directed me into this building with a sign in front that read "University of the Nations." Below this, a sign read, "Youth with a Mission."

Four years ago, the Lord told me that I would one day travel the world and speak to thousands of people. I had no idea how all of this was to come about but here I was, going to an unknown place, a library, for what?

I need to back up a little and tell you how my life has changed since I have accepted the Lord into my life and heart. . I went into the Marine Corps at eighteen years old, feeling it was my patriotic duty. My two brothers, Bill and George, were in Vietnam at the time; this also served as further inspiration to join the military. Seven months after I entered into the service, my brother Bill was discharged from the Marines. My brother George stayed in Vietnam for another seven years. I, on the other hand, went to Okinawa. I stayed there walking Satan's path. I did every illegal thing possible!

Being in charge of processing, I had the sad job of sending marines to Vietnam and a more pleasant experience of sending marines back home. Interestingly, the expressions on the faces of the marines leaving their duty were much sadder than the ones arriving. Therefore, being the sinner that I am, I found that I could let marines headed home out of the service early, upon arriving back in the States…for a price! I could also hold marines in Okinawa, by losing their records for a few months, this also for a price. I had justified and rationalized my behavior for my monetary benefit. Looking back, knowing what I now know of God, I realize I was just as sad and unhappy as many of the other brothers. My guilt and sadness permeated my being on a daily basis. As a result, I turned to drugs and alcohol to numb my negative reality.

When the C.I.D. (military intelligence) became aware of marines being discharged and detained improperly, I became a suspect, and the C.I.D. proceeded to search my locker. They found nothing to prove my guilt, but I knew if I did not leave, they would eventually find out what had been happening.

I made the decision to do what I had set out to do from the beginning: I changed my records around to what I felt would be my last flight, a flight to Vietnam. I did not see my brother, George, because he was now in Saigon. I was in charge of bunkers covering the Da Nang airstrip.

On my way home from Vietnam, I had to stop in Okinawa again to change flights. I went into my old office and realized that I now had the look on my face that I had seen so many thousand times before on the faces of the marines returning home. I was no longer the same person I was when I left Okinawa.

As I was getting on the plane to go home, I thought about a marine who should have been with me. He was a good man but he had received a "Dear John" letter about a week before. We left the bunkers by helicopter to go the Da Nang airport. In the helicopter, each of us was in our own thoughts about what the future held. We were all very quiet. All of sudden, this buddy of mine unsnapped his seat belt, stood up, and with tears in his eyes, he ran to the back of the helicopter and jumped.

Each of us sat devastatingly stunned and crying, while some prayed. I felt I would never feel the extreme pain I felt at that moment. I was wrong. I arrived home to a town, a country where the people displayed hate instead of love. I felt totally lost, depressed, and potentially suicidal. I knew now why men had re-enlisted for second and third tours.

I will stop here and refrain from writing about all the sinful things I did over the past twenty years. I wanted you to have an idea of what my life was like before I arrived to this point and why I am writing now.

Four years and four months ago, I was discharged from an AA rehabilitation center in Sheraton, Wyoming. I moved to Hawaii to be with family members and try to find what had been lost the last twentytwo years.

I would go to the beach each day after work and sit on the pier. Each day, I would sit and talk with whom I thought was God. Each day, I felt there was a reason for my being at the pier. I would say, "Lord, I know I am supposed to be here for some reason. One of these days I know you will show me."

One day as I was leaving this pier, I saw a homeless woman lying on a bench. She seemed to be very poor and old, I felt, because of the way she was dressed and because of the many wrinkles on her face. As I walked by, I stopped to put some money in her coat pocket, so she could buy something to eat when she awoke. As I was walking away from her, a young woman came up to me to say what a wonderful thing it was that I had done. After introducing one another, she asked if I was a born-again Christian. I asked what she meant by that and she said, "Have you ever been saved? Have you asked the Lord for forgiveness of your sins?"

My first thought was, here you go again, Bob; you have another one of those holy rollers on your back. Then, I thought that maybe this is what I had been waiting for all this time on the pier. This is what the Lord wants me to hear. I opened my heart that night. Ruth, my new found friend, and I sat on the beach until three thirty in the morning talking about God. We then went to have breakfast until I had to go to work. The next few days went very slowly. I wanted Sunday to come so badly. I was hungry to have what she had, so much so, I drove my friends and co-workers crazy.

When I walked into the Word of Life Church and heard the singing and clapping, I felt right at home. I prayed that morning with all my heart. I said, "Lord, if you want me to come into your world, you'll have to hit me over the head with a hammer". I cried hard when I asked him to come into my life that morning. The next evening, Ruth and I went to the zoo. While sitting in the parking lot, all of a sudden I had an intense feeling to get out of the car. The Lord was talking to me. It was just as if there was a voice in my head. It was clear and kind. He told me of my life and why I had lived the life, I had. I could go into more detail but it would take a very long time. He talked to me all night as I walked along the beach. The next day, he kept on going. I couldn't do my work. I could not paint and listen at the same time. My brother must have thought I was going crazy when I told them I had to be alone to listen to what God was telling me. The most important thing he said was, "One day, you will travel the world and you'll be speaking to thousands of people. You will help the young, the old, the homeless, and the veterans. You will be spreading my word like no one has heard before."

During this time, it was as if I was not here on earth. My body was, but my soul and heart were in heaven, if this is possible to imagine. It is as if there was complete peace in my whole body. The most beautiful feeling anyone could hope for, and ten times more so. I could not possibly explain exactly how I felt but I know I did not want it to ever end. I was truly in heaven here on earth. I now understood how life was supposed to be, not my way, but His way. He said, "In five years, you will start to walk my path." At the time, I did not know why I would wait five-years. I did know that it was truth, and he had his reasons, so I didn't try to figure out why.

Approximately one month later, my best friend, my Vietnam brother, and blood brother all in one, George, died in a veteran's hospital in Seattle. The Lord had told me that I would feel great pain and sorrow soon. At the time, I never could have imagined that it would be so extreme.

I went back to drinking, getting into fights, and being in and out of hospitals. At one time, I had three doctors who couldn't and wouldn't let me die. I almost did die three times. I saw the worst part of life every minute of the day, for almost four years. When I was in the hospital the last time, the doctors told my family that if I left the hospital this time on my own and with out their permission, that I would die if I continued the self-abuse. I was unaware that the doctors had spoken to my family. I stayed in the hospital for two more days. On the third morning, I asked the Lord what I was going to do. Not a few moments later, the phone rang; it was my brother on the Big Island of Hawaii. He asked me if I would like to come over and stay with him for a while. I had known that he had a couple of strokes, so I thought he needed me for support. I felt that this was the answer to my prayers. Three hours later, I was on a plane. When I was getting ready to leave, boththe nurse and doctor advised me not to leave. They said I was not ready, that I had many problems, and they could help if I stayed. I knew the Lord wanted me to go, and so far, each time I had trusted Him He always came through for me.

On January 15, 1995, I left for the Big Island, and I haven't had a drink or done anything against God's will since then. After staying with my brother for three weeks, I was told to go to Kailua-Kona. This is where I started to see God's plan, which is why I started this letter to you.

I went up the driveway of these buildings and went into the main office, where I asked if they had a library. I didn't know what I was looking for, but I remember asking the Lord how I could learn to pray the right way, just a few hours earlier. As I walked to the library, I crossed over a lot and up a stairway. When I reached the top, there in the center was a huge water fountain. All around this fountain were flags of every nation, standing about thirty feet high. It was an overwhelming sight to see. I walked into the library and asked for a book on praying.

She took me to a shelf and I reached out for a book, unknowingly chose a book with the title, God and I. The book was old. The seams were unglued in many areas. I checked it out anyway. I knew that this was the book I was to read. I never in my life found such a wonderful, fulfilling, and honest book.

Iverna, I have learned more from your book, and received more answers than I ever could have found by myself, thank God. I just cannot thank the Lord enough to express the knowledge that I now have, by your writing. He has given you a wonderful talent, a talent, that I am sure has helped many people. Thank you for walking His path. I know the joy I have felt when God spoke to me, heaven here on earth, and I see that same joy expressed in your writings.

I now live in a clean and sober home. I will soon be moving into an apartment alone. The Lord has been guiding me in many ways and I trust I will be attending the University of the Nations in his name. I hope to achieve this by selling my innovative walking canes, the top handles made into shapes of whales or dolphins. I believe these will be a great item for not only the elderly but also, the beachgoer and hiker.

Everything I do now seems to come out positively. I feel lifted from the heaviness I once experienced, and I feel blessed in every way. The opportunity to be able to read your writings, and write to you in thanks has put a close to one chapter in my life and a new beginning in the light of God.

I will close with "If you have to search for the pot of gold at the end of the rainbow, you don't have a pot of gold with in your heart." This phrase came from a book I wrote for my mother on Mother's Day. One of an Even Dozen was the title of the book. Interestingly, the phrase came from my heart, but it was not until knowing God that I knew who the true author was. The phrase simply means, if you are going through life searching for the big money, the house, car, and other material things in life, then you are not walking in the path of the Lord. However, if you are helping others to find peace with in and can help them in any way possible for the Lord, you are no longer searching. I have my pot of gold with in my heart, and it is walking the Lord's path. I am a truly happy man today! Thank the Lord and thank you! I hope to meet you or hear from you someday.

God Bless You,

Robert Dunham

Iverna Tompkins Letter and Reply

"The Righteous Are Bold As A Lion"
Iverna Tompkins Ministries
P.O. Box 30427
Phoenix, Arizona 85046
Phone 602-443-8001
Fax 602-443-8004

November 21, 1995

"Songs of the Children"
Bob Dunham

Dear Robert,

What an incredible blessing your letter is to me. I am thrilled at what God is doing in your life and so delighted to have been a little part of it.

It is obvious that God has much that is wonderful in store for you and I rejoice with you in the vision He has given you that will keep you as it did Paul, who said, "I am not disobedient in the heavenly vision." It is wonderful how He provides not only motivation but that continuing light moving on ahead to keep us going when things around us are dark. I believe you have set your feet on His pathway and they shall not be moved.

I am, of course, so appreciative of YWAM. I have had the good fortune to share with them at different times and love their vision. I also consider David Rees-Thomas, who has a church there, as a personal friend. I hope you will be able to receive from him not only his knowledge of the Word, but his loving and gracious spirit, so filled with the Holy Spirit.

I am enclosing a copy of God and I so you may have your own copy as well as another one of my books that I hope will be a blessing to you. We do have a free lending library of tapes if that is something that would be of service to you.

I pray God will bring revelation of His truth, found you firmly on His Word, fill you with His joy and delight you with His love.

Abiding in His love,

Iverna

Aloha, Pastor Iverna, my sister in the Lord, and friend always,

I wanted to give you an update of my past since last we touched one another, by the grace of God, our Father. I have been praying for your healthand peace with in. I hope all is going as God has planned for you and all of your loved ones.

I think I sent you a letter or called you and thanked you for the books. In case I did not, I wish to say, "Thank You" now, and tell you that I enjoyed them immensely. I also wanted to send you things that I have been writing. I have many more but they are in storage. These are the most recent ones.

I had the pleasure of seeing you on TV today. You look spunky and happy as ever I saw you. Keep up the good work, my friend. Isn't it wonderful how not only does God keep us young at heart but some of you are blessed with staying youthful looking!

I also saw Joyce Meyer here at the Blaisdell Center last week. She is a wonderful child of God, isn't she, Iverna? She spoke of many things that I enjoyed and I wrote a letter to her. I gave it to someone to give to her. I added to the letter some of the things that I have also sent to you. I pray she received them. Ruth brought the book, *How to Hear from God,* while we were there. I read it right away and found it filled with answers. The Lord told me that one day I would meet her. I plan also to meet with you one day. Only the Lord knows when, but I feel strongly that it will happen. I truly look forward to that day as well, my friend.

I will not take up any more of your busy time. I would like to tell you that my wife, Ruth, and I are now living in Honolulu. We love it here but we sure miss the Big Island. It was by the grace of God, however, that I was able to help so many on the Big Island. Ruth was with me all the way and I feel blessed to have her in my life.

If you should ever happen to be coming to Honolulu, Ruth and I sure would enjoy taking you and your guest out for breakfast, lunch, or dinner (or all of the above).

Please stay in touch. I have made friends with two ministers now, the Reverend Lew Schaffer of Son Shine Ministries in Azle, Texas, and now you. I write to Brother Lew all the time. He is such a wonderful person and a true child of God, our Father. I had the chance to fly over to Minnesota a few years back and stopped in at Son Shine and spent a few days with them. What a great outreach they have. They travel the world and just recently, Rev. Lew said it would be very nice indeed to travel to another country with one another. I would be blessed to have that come true soon. God is so good; I just never know what to expect.

I was wondering if I sent to you a film I once made with a small testament on it. If I did not, I would be happy to share it with you.

I must stop taking up so much of your time. Thank you very much for all that you have done for so many of God's children and those that are lost. You are a blessing to my wife and me. Please stay the way you are, but, if you choose to change, may it keep getting better and fuller with God's love and blessings.

"We love you, but we could never love you as much as He does".

Brother Bob and Sister Ruth.

Pray About Everything

Aloha family, friends and all of God's children,

Are you a good person, a friend, a child of God, walking to be all that you can be on the Lord's path? Do you know anyone like this person? Are you such a person? Maybe I can help you if you are struggling for an answer.

Whether you are any of the above, you are on the right path and God has hope for you. However, you must do your part and that starts with a positive attitude. A very dear person to my heart, Pastor Iverna Tompkins, once responded to a letter I had written to her with these words:

> *"It is obvious that God has much that is wonderful in store for you and I rejoice with you in the vision He has given you that will keep you as it did Paul, who said, 'I am not disobedient in the heavenly vision.' It is wonderful how He provides not only motivation but also that continuing light moving on ahead to keep us going when things around us are dark. I believe you have set your feet on His pathway and they shall not be moved."*

I share with you what she wrote to me, not for my own ego, but more reason than ever to be humble. Let me explain: I was going through many difficult things in my life before I wrote to Pastor Iverna, such as having just come off the streets with an alcohol disease after having been homeless for thirteen years. I was very negative and selfish. I had no desire to think positive when all that I saw around me was a very negative world. However, I found no reason whatsoever to think negatively once I gave my life to the Lord and accepted Jesus as my personal savior. He took away the negative when He died on the cross.

Therefore, coming from a person who has "been out there," I speak with all humbleness when I say that I know what you are going through. I have been to places and have done things that most men would never go through if they had three lives to live. I am not comparing myself to Paul, but I could run a close second in life's hardships. I tell you this so you will be more attentive to what I wish to convey to you in this message. I am no better than you, nor am I any worse. That is because I have this kind of love in my heart for you that is so strong that you cannot cut it with a knife if you wished to. I do not have to know you personally to know that there is some goodness in you. I am well aware that there are those who have gone over the edge or feel they have. However, I believe that all men and women have good hearts.

The late great actor and politician, Will Rogers, once said, "There isn't a man I ever met that I didn't like for one reason or another." He was right in saying that. I feel the same way. Most people will reach out to others, but when you know the Lord, it goes much deeper than just reaching out. You feel from the heart the pain that a complete stranger feels, if you have also died on the cross with Jesus. His love was, "everything" that He could give to us. His love was so strong that He gave His life for us. He gave just as the commandment says, "Love your neighbor with all your heart and soul." The best thing that any man can do for another is to give his life for whomever, as Jesus did for us.

Why not have a positive attitude toward your fellow man? Show your love to one another just as Jesus showed His love for us and you cannot help but feel anything less than love.

Here are six things to do daily to keep your life in order and have peace with those around you, because love is peace after all:

1. Think positively about everything
2. Study the Word
3. Thank God for His grace
4. Have patience and faith
5. Pray about everything
6. Listen for answered prayer

Of these six things, I keep, "praying about everything" on the top of the list. I pray before I read the Bible. I have faith that my prayers will be answered. I wait faithfully, and with patience, then I will soon hear His answer. I then thank Him for His grace, His unconditional love, and His bestowing upon me a positive attitude. Praise is to God.

I pray that I was of help to you in some small way. If not, "pray about it."

"I love you, but I could never love you as much as He does".

Brother Bob

Joyce Meyer Ministries, Letter One

Joyce Meyer Ministries
P.O. Box 655 · FENTON, MO 63026 ·(636) 349-0303
www.joycemeyer.org

January 23, 2004

Robert Dunham
P.O. BOX 8967
Honolulu, Hawaii 96830-0967

Dear Robert,

We wanted to take a moment to express our joy in your victory. Testimonies like yours keep us pressing on and encourage us in those times when we need it most.

We know that God is able to complete whatever concerns you and your loved ones. We encourage you to continue in your spiritual growth, staying close to the Lord in fellowship, as He removes the spots and wrinkles from your life and prepares you to be His bride.

Once again, thank you for taking the time to share your heart and your victory with us. We will continue to press on in every good work by preaching the Gospel through every available avenue until the return of our blessed Lord and Savior, Jesus Christ. We send our love.

We care about you,

Dave and Joyce Meyer

A Letter to a Child in Christ

Aloha Nadun, "Happy Birthday,"

I just happened to write this little story this morning on the following page. (The John Newton Story) I was thinking to myself this morning, "why did God have me write this story?' Then, when I went to the mailbox, I found your letter in it. Therefore, I believe the Lord wanted you to read this story for some reason. Maybe you will be a sailor and help people to reach their new home. On the other hand, maybe, you will be a great captain one day, sailing the high seas with many other sailors, helping some country out that is in a war of some kind. Whatever the reason for you to receive this story, God does have a reason and one day you will know what it is. Maybe you should save this letter and this story, and one day, look back and say to yourself, "that's why God had me read the story."

I feel that one day we will meet, Nadun. Ruth and I are praying that we do, anyway. I have much to tell you. I have some stories for you that will make you laugh, cry, and feel blessed. Here is another one for you as a sample:

There once was a young man (we will call him Sam), who at eighteen years young, wanted to travel. Therefore, he went into the U.S. Marine Corps. Another reason he joined the marines was that he had another brother who was also an marine. He had a brother who was in the army, as well. However, after boot camp, he found out that the only place he would be traveling was to Vietnam. Therefore, off he went to war. When he came back from Vietnam, he was a changed person. He was not the eighteen-years-young man any more. He was now twenty years young and he wanted to go to college. He went into college in California, and after a year and a half, he thought he wanted to travel more instead of going to college.

That opportunity came when he met a man who drove a truck for a moving company. The man said he moved furniture across the United States for a major truck company. Sam saw this as his chance to go around the whole country. Sam and his new friend started out in a town called Riverside, California. They were soon crossing the big state of Texas, on and on they went. Sam was having the time of his life. He saw things he had always read about and saw pictures of in books.

Then one day, a sad thing happened to Sam. Sam and his new friend arrived into the state of NorthCarolina. It was late, dark outside, and they felt like stopping at a diner for some food. After they ordered their food and ate it up, they wanted to play some pool on the pool table that was in the diner. They were having a great time. Sam's friend was also happy because a girl came into the diner that he had met before on one of his previous trips to NorthCarolina.

After about an hour and a half, Sam's friend said he would be back soon. His friend said that he and the girl were going somewhere to see other folks. Sam waited and waited for his friend to come back, but he never did. The diner was going to close and Sam had to leave. The truck that they had been traveling in was at least thirty miles away. Sam wasn't even sure if he could find it. Nevertheless, he had no choice but to look for it so he started to hitchhike. It was about 2:00 am and there were very few cars on the road. They parked way outside of the city and it was dark as coal for miles and miles. As Sam walked along, he would think about all the things he had seen so far in his travels. He then saw a car coming toward him from a great distance. "Maybe this person will stop," thought Sam. He had seen only two cars in the last two hours. As the car came closer, Sam began to wave his arms hoping the car would see him and stop. The car slowed down and to Sam's delight, stopped.

When Sam opened the car door, he felt happy that this person was kind enough to stop. As he sat down in the front seat, he looked over at the man. Sam saw that this man was huge. This stranger had arms on him the size of none Sam had ever seen before, Sam thought to himself. "This guy looks like Samson". (Samson in the Bible). Not only were his arms huge, but also the rest of him was too. "This guy must be six feet four inches tall, and he could be trouble; he's way too big for me to beat up in a fight," were the things going through Sam's mind as they started to drive down the road.

The stranger asked Sam where he was going and Sam told him he wasn't sure. Sam told the man that all he was sure of is that the truck he rode in was along the highway they were on. After driving for about an hour, they came upon the truck. The truck had a full load of furniture and Sam thought that maybe he should not have told this stranger that. This stranger could be a thief and Sam could be robbed. When they had come to a stop and Sam got out, the stranger did also. This did not worry Sam too much because he didn't have the keys to the inside of the truck anyway. As Sam walked over to open the side door of the truck where he slept, he all of a sudden felt those big hands of the stranger around his throat. The man picked up Sam and threw him into the truck as if he were as light as a feather. The stranger was not slow on his feet either; he was up off his feet and in the truck before Sam could turn around. The stranger then began to tear Sam's pants off.

Sam had to think fast. He knew from experience in other fights that this ape had the advantage already. "What am I to do if I want to stay alive and get out of this?" Sam thought. As the man started to take Sam's pants down Sam tried to wrap his hands around the ape's throat. Sam saw, when he tried this that his hands looked like the hands of a doll around the man's neck. His hands were too small to choke this gorilla. Now Sam knew he was about to be killed or raped, or both.

Sam did not pray for help; he didn't want to have any help. You see, Sam was angry. He had just been to a war. He had been one of twelve children whose dad never had time for him. When he came home from Vietnam, the people in his country spit on him and called him a baby killer. Sam had always had to go through life on his own. He did not want anyone to help because no one could. If ever there was a sad man in life with enough anger for ten men, it was Sam. "I'm on my own," he thought.

As Sam grabbed the man by the throat, he said to the stranger, "Listen, you piece of ____, if you don't get out right now, you're dead." Sam knew that if he couldn't scare this man, he would be dead.

As Sam tightened his grip, the stranger looked into Sam's eyes and with a grin on his face, he said, "I can break you like a twig."

Sam had to think faster than ever he had before. He said, with tears in his eyes, "Listen, I'm sorry, but I have hemorrhoids and there is no way you're going to be able to do anything to me. I swear to God, I got them from all this heavy lifting on the job."

It worked. The man believed him. The stranger got up and pulled up his pants. Now Sam thought to himself, "Is he going to kill me? No, he seems to be pretty calm, I have to keep talking." Then Sam said to the man, with tears in his eyes, "Could you do me a favor and give me a few dollars so I can get some food tomorrow? My friend took off with some girl and I haven't been paid yet."

"I've fooled him all the way now", Sam thought to himself. The man reached into his back pocket and took out his wallet. He took out eight dollars and gave it to Sam. Sam told him he was very grateful and that he was happy he could eat now. The man then got in his car and took off.

Sam never told his friend about what happened that night when he woke up the next morning. In fact, Sam was twenty-two then and he never told that story to anyone for another twenty-two years. Sam was in the nut ward, in a veteran's hospital, because of a seizure he had when he lived out on the streets. (The Doctor was a shrink, Psychologist, and he talked Sam into telling him the story. You see, Sam was an alcoholic and a drug addict soon after that happened. Sam was homeless for thirteen years. He went through seven girlfriends and his family wanted nothing to do with him. None of his brothers and sisters wanted him around because he was always drunk. Sam trusted no one. No one knew why. However, Sam knew the reason he was always on guard: "trust no one" was his motto ever since he was a boy.

You may be wondering why I am sending a story like this. It is because we must all learn to trust in someone or something. If we trust no one, we are lost and alone, just as Sam was alone. Who better to trust in than the Lord himself? Please read and follow through in your life by way of the Ten Commandments, Nadun. Sam did the best he knew how; however, he did not know God or the Ten Commandments.

I am sure you are curious why I said Sam did his best. Well, as you have probably already figured out, Nadun, I am "Sam." I did the best I knew how to live life, but I was doing it alone. After forty-five years of struggles, I turned my life over to the Lord. I asked God for His help. In fact, the Lord spoke to me audibly and told me many wonderful things that He would have me do. First, the Lord said, I would have to suffer yet another four years of pain. However, the fifthyear, the Lord had said, I would begin to do His works. I am very happy to say that since I asked God for help, I have been able to help many homeless men and women on the Hawaiian Islands with clothing, food, and shelter. I am studying daily to be all that I can be for our Father in heaven. Praise is to God. I am married, as you know, and my wife and I are bothvery happy together ministering the Lord's word with all who will listen. We try to live by the Ten Commandments as much as possible. Everyone has a story, Nadun. One day, God willing, I will send you a copy of the book I plan to write. It is all God's timing. In the mean time, please try to live, "One day at time".

If ever you should feel the urge to give up, Nadun, call on the Lord. If He should tell you to contact me for any reason whatever, do not hesitate to do so. Do it anyway. I would love to hear from you.

I hope you have enjoyed my story. Please write or send another picture soon. We love you, Nadun, but we could never love you as much as He does.

Words of wisdom from a brother of mine, in the Lord, and a reverend, "Pray about everything," listen, and always, always, do as the Lord tells you.

"We love you, but we could never love you as much as He does"..

Brother Bob and Sister Ruth

How Sweet Thou Are

Slavery in the 1800s was a very lucrative business. One slave trader that I have read about was John Newton. Maybe you have heard his name before, but in case you have not, I would like to give you a quick review of his life.

John Newton was a slave himself at one time. After a short time on one ship as a slave, he was, sold to another ship's captain who was also in the slave trade. John stayed on this captain's ship until he was twenty three. That year he also became a slave trader.

However, back at home in England, he had left a young woman behind who he loved dearly. She was a Christian woman who had once told John that she could not marry him, as much as she desired to do however, because John was not a Christian and had no wish to be one. John explained to his sweetheart that when he was a young boy of six, his mother died and he could find no reason to believe in God if God cared not for his mother.

However, before John left for his journey on the high seas, Mary, his sweetheart, asked John to take a little book with him to read on the ship. Even though John told Mary he had no time to read because of the hard labor, he decided it would please her if he did so.

After many slave-trading trips across the ocean, John decided to read his books. One of the books was the book Mary had given Him. His men often chided him about the time he spent reading. Some came to believe that maybe he would start to get holy with them one day. However, when asked why he read so often, John would simply say he wished to know why people believed in God.

When off the coast of Ireland, and about to be home to England soon, the men and their ship came upon a terrible storm. Surely, they would all die if the storm did not pass soon. As the waves increased in size and men were going overboard, Captain John looked to the sky and said, "If you are up there, we sure could use your help now."

After a day and a night of fighting the waves, the storm stopped. The first mate came to the captain and said that all the men were speaking of how well he had handled the ship. They were very grateful for his strength at the wheel, for the captain stayed the course for the entire time. The captain then said, “It was not I alone at the helm, Stymie.” The first mate asked the captain why he said that. “It was God who took us through the storm” was the reply of the Captain.

When the ship reached England, John went to see his loved one. He asked Mary if he could ask her father for her hand in marriage. After John told the story of how God had saved the ship at sea, John had also told Mary he had given his life to the Lord. Mary said her father would be no problem to him. After all, Mary’s father only wished for her to be with the man she loved, and that man was now a Christian.

You may think that the story would end there, but it does not. You see, John sailed for three more trips selling slaves. John still had not learned that God did not wish for him to sell other human beings. After those three trips, John settled down in London as a designer of sea trafficking and routes to the many lands he had sailed. He also came to realize that what he had done in his life was not the way of God. John saw that he had a talent for writing books and poems. One day, he went to Mary and said he would like her opinion on his latest poem. The poem started out like this, “I once was lost, but now I’m found, was blind, but now I see..”

By the grace of God, John Newton had been saved. By the Grace of God, so am I. John Newton, a one-time slave trader, wrote the song “Amazing Grace” while at sea in storming weather. Should you decide to give your life to God, what may He have in store for you? Do not wait for the hard time to come before you ask our Father for his help. Ask him today and find out just what he has in store for you in the years to come. Many people are too stubborn to ask for help; I was. Nevertheless, when I did ask, I stopped drinking and got off the street. Because I asked Him for help, He gave me life.

8/16/03
I love you, but I could never love you as much as He does..

Brother Bob

Hiding around the Corner

5/15/04

Aloha family, friends and all of God's children,

Many times in my life, and I believe in other's lives as well, we want to go and hide around the corner. Alternatively, we want to hide under the bed, run to the hills, and "get out of Dodge." Running was my way of escape. I didn't know at the time that I was running. I thought, "What the hell do I have to put up with this crap for?" Then I would head for the highway. The only time I ever ran (other than being on foot while hitchhiking) was when I stole a car up in Seattle.

Kathy (the partner I hooked up with in a California park), and I hitched a ride up the coast. It was wintertime and all we had was a bag each with one set of clothes to keep warm. We did not think about how bad it was going to be going through the mountains. When you are an alcoholic, you don't think; you just say, "To hell with everything, let's go." That is a fact. I did it for fourteen years. You have only a certain degree of common sense and heart. It matters not how intelligent you are when you're a boozer; with booze, you lose. However, I didn't care about myself or anyone else. To a certain degree, you care for those you love, but the bottle comes first. I knew I did not care, but my heart would take much suffering and pain before realizing the answer to everyone's question, "What is life all about?"

By the time Kathy and I reached Redmond, California, we bothwere sick and had colds. I thought Kathy might get pneumonia, if she did not already have it. After being in the rain, sleet, and freezing cold for six hours, I had to get us a place out of the cold. Therefore, when I saw the house that looked vacant, just on the outskirts of town, I broke the door open. It was empty. There was no furniture, so we lay down in a corner. We were out of the rain, but we still had the shivers. By morning, with very little sleep, we hit the road again. That is when Kathy said she had written a song. When I asked her what it was about, she said it was about me. Then she said the title was, "A Man with a Heart of Silver and Gold." She started to sing it and I thought it was going to bring tears to my eyes. I had no idea that this woman was so in love with me.

When we made it to Seattle, two days later, I did not want to go to my family for help. I knew that I could get help but I was the kind of man who just could not ask for that kind of help. I would rather sleep in an abandoned car before I would let my brothers see me like this. That is what we did. I knew a person who had an auto repair shop and we went to see him. He said he didn't have a place for us to sleep, but if we wanted to, we could sleep in a vacant VW van. It started to snow and we really did not have much choice.

We lived in that van for four months. The plus side of our stay there is that there was a social services building nearby, and Kathy was able to get her teethfixed. She was also able to get welfare. Therefore, we had a little drinking money. I worked on some odd jobs here and there. None of my friends wanted to see me once they heard I was in town. They wanted nothing to do with me once they heard through the grapevine that I was on a life time drinking plan. One day, I did go to see my parents. This was before Kathy had her teethfixed and her hair styled. Therefore, I did not take Kathy up with me. When I walked into their home, there sat two brothers I had not expected to see. I saw Dennis first, sitting across the room. Then my brother, Roger, walked up and said, "Hey, Bob, got a surprise for you." Roger pointed to something or someone around the corner.

As I walked around to see what he was talking about, there sat my brother, George, whom I had not seen in about a year and a half. Although I had not seen Dennis in almost three years and I had just met his new wife, I gave all of my attention to George. For years, I had much remorse for being so indignant to Dennis. I asked Dennis and George to come downstairs to meet someone. I didn't tell them I had a woman with me. When we went outside, I introduced them to Kathy. Kathy and George hit it off right away. Dennis was being Dennis, kind of shy and quiet. We talked for about five or ten minutes and they left. As I look back at those few short minutes, I realize now how embarrassed my brothers were for me.

George would later tell me, "Bob, you have had some pretty tough and hardcore women in your life, but this one has them all beat."

I said to him in response, "If you think she looks rough, just think how the women in prison felt when she walked in with them. She was sent up for murder."

George laughed until I told him I was serious. George asked me, "Did you break her out of jail?" We bothlaughed so hard we could hardly stand on our feet. (We bothknew that the way that I was living anything was possible.)

Then, I — in all seriousness— said, "Yes."

After the laughter stopped, I told him what had been happening since last we met. One thing about George is that he never once gave his opinion unless I asked for it first. He respected me and I him. However, I knew he was concerned about my life so in order to avoid being the "big brother," he stayed clear of me while I stayed in Seattle. Everyone did. Everyone who knew me was scared to confront me about what was happening to me. They either were afraid of confrontation, which would have lead to a fistfight, or they just could not deal with it. I was on my own. I wanted it that way anyway. I didn't need anyone. I was my own man. I was going to prove that society did not run my life. Therefore, I stuck my head around the corner once again.

After being in Seattle for those few months, I started to get bored again. One night, we went to a bar a few blocks away to get drunk, our favorite pastime. I saw a few people I had known from the past. One of them I couldn't remember other than by his face. I could not remember much of anything or anybody in those days. However, this fellow and I had quite a few laughs through the night. He told me how he had to give up his wife, but not why. I wanted to change the subject so I said, "Jack [or whatever his name was] do you think I could borrow your car and take Kathy down to the Government Locks [a tourist site]?" I then told him she had not seen anything since we arrived into town. He said, "Listen, Bob, I have all my tools in the truck. I sleep in it and I have to have that car in order to get to work and survive. If you are sure you can drive all right, I do not care. But make sure you bring it back soon because I have to work early."

I walked over to Kathy and told her we were going sightseeing. Before we left, we went over to thank "Jack." When we started to pull out of the driveway of the bar parking lot, I watched to see if anyone was following. That was just an old habit of mine. However, to my surprise, I did see a car following us. That made me mad. It was nice of Jack's friends to care about him and his car, but I was insulted about it.

As we neared the Government Locks, I asked Kathy, "What do you say we take off for California right now?"

She laughed and said, "How do you plan to do that, Bob? Steal a car or steal money?"

I told her, "Jack is having us followed or his friends are doing it because they don't trust me."

Kathy asked me if I would really take a friend's car. She reminded me that Jack needed the car for work and she thought it would be a rotten thing to do to him.

I said, "Well, if Jack's friends love him enough to follow me, then they love him enough to buy him a new car and some tools." I turned a nice easy turn. I saw them turn behind me so now I knew this was not my imagination, I started to speed up. At first, it looked like I was just picking up a little speed. However, what I was doing was making an escape plan in my head. I know Seattle like the back of my hand, so I knew these men would be easy to lose. I lost them with in four blocks. It was like taking candy from a baby. Only I was taking away a man's livelihood, his home, and his only possessions.

As I was losing these guys, I flashed back to a time when I was hitchhiking in Washington, years earlier. This very big, rough-looking person picked me up. The inside of his car was all beat up. Missing stereo, buttons on the panel missing, broken windows, etc. It's interior was destroyed. I asked him what happened to his car and he said in a real angry voice, "A man should be a man and come to you one-on-one when he is pissed off at you. Instead, some assholes took it out on my car. It is like in the old days; when the best thing a man had was his horse. This car is the best thing I own and some bastard tears it apart. I would rather he stole it than to tear it apart."

I started to laugh aloud as we turned onto the freeway ramp. Kathy asked me what was so funny, so I told her that story.

She said, "I wonder why it is that men have such a thing about their cars."

I thought about it a moment and said, "I think a man's car is kind of like his woman. If he has a good one, he likes to touch her up, feel every part of her, make her shine, and brag about her. If another man touches it, they're in big trouble. If another man tries to take her away, he will fight for her. Sometimes, men are very possessive. If it came to a choice — his woman or his car — he does not put one before the other because then he would have to give up his woman. Jack just lost his car. He will feel like he lost more now than when he gave up his woman." She laughed hard about my explanation of the choice between the two.

While traveling down to California, I had time to think about what I just did to "Jack." At that time in my life, I had remorse about many things that happened in Seattle. Not just in Seattle, but for the previous thirty-one years, as well. I felt so much guilt. Maybe, in fact now that I see those years on the sober side of the bridge, I stayed drunk to cover over the guilt. The sadness, the sorrow, and heartache that I caused in other lives were just too unbearable to go through sober. Nevertheless, I would only lose the pain as long as the drunk lasted. When I was sober, it all would come back and I would go back to my best friend, the bottle.

I would, one day, years later, give my best friend a burial. He was at half mass (or half full). I was under a bridge in Hawaii, feeling like the world was about to collapse, and I blamed it all on him. Therefore, I told him we had to part. I started to cry as I dug his grave with a piece of wood. I was sobbing profusely as I lay him in his grave. Then I said a prayer for him. I said, "My friend, we been though a lot of hard times but it's time to part." (Sniff, sniff.) I was very serious. I was hurting bad. We had been best friends for almost thirty years. There was a person on a motorcycle about twenty feet away, watching me bury my friend, and he did not know what to think about this picture.

I just ignored the stranger and went on saying my good-bye, "Buddy, if I could give my own life for you, I would. (Sniff, sniff.) But you know as well as me that this has got to end here and now." (Sniff, sniff.) I lay him down in his grave and covered him up. Then, I walked over to the person watching me as I wiped the tears from my eyes, and said, "Listen, man, when I come back here, I do not want to see this grave disturbed at all. You understand that this was very hard for me to do. He was my best friend and I sure would not want your best friend's grave to be dug up. OK?"

He looked at me as if to say, "Oh yeah, I understand." (However, he wasn't crying.) Then he said he wouldn't touch it. I walked away feeling like I had made the right decision. There was some pain, sure, but I knew I would have to deal with it.

When I came back two hours later to bring my friend back to life, he was gone. I never would have expected there to be grave robbers in Hawaii. Therefore, I went to pick up his brother. (He has many brothers. :-) (This is how this alcoholic used to think. Sick.)

I joke now, but I sure felt for "Jack." If ever I have enough money, I am going to find that person and buy him a car and new tools. What did I learn from this story, upon reflection? Well, there are many things. However, I would have to break it down to one thing, which is this: "Because I can now take what comes my way, I owe it all to Jesus. Where once I could not stand, I am upright. And, with the Lord in my heart, I have no need to run, hide around the corner, or head for the hills. With Jesus for you, who can be against you?"

"I love you, but I could never love you as much as He does."

Brother Bob

Tired of My Mistakes

Aloha, family, friends, and all of God's children,

As you know, I start writing at four in the morning. However, what I didn't tell you is that I fall asleep sometimes when reading. That is because after working outdoors all day, then coming in the house to read and write for three or four hours, I get tired out. Maybe I should not get up so early. The reason I am telling you this is that I started to study for my bachelor's degree from Masters of Divinity School home study. One of the things I love about this studying is that I can be listening to tapes for four hours and it seems like only ten minutes.

Studying did not come easy for me when I was a young man. I was in the, "in crowd," and in order to hang with some friends of mine, I had to prove myself. Therefore, I would go with them to football games and we would fight the students from that school just to prove that we were tougher than they were. We would go to the Seattle Center where the Space Needle and all the rides were. Ferris wheel, games, girls, and fighting came with the adventure.

However, as I look back, I see we were nothing more than just young punks. We hung out with all of the prettiest girls in school, drank beer, and did whatever we felt like doing. Later, I started to do drugs, all the time thinking how cool I was. I could tell you some things that I did that I was proud of in those days, like stopping one of my friends from putting another kid in the hospital or possibly killing him. On the other hand, I could tell you about how I had won so many girls over but I stopped fooling myself long ago. When I was young, I had bad teethand the girls just did not think much of that. However, they did like the charm I displayed.

I did not win girls over; I used them. I didn't save that other kid's life when I helped him; I only stopped myself from going to prison. Being, "cool with the in crowd," is not what I thought it was after all. We were just some little punks taking advantage of girls and ganging up on those less likely to hurt us in a fight. I was a fool. I would be too tired to study or I would come home and pass out. That meant, of course, that I would fail and not pass on to the next grade level. I did not and so I quit school when I was seventeen. I could not find work because I quit school, and for that reason (plus being caught with my neighbor's wife), I joined the U.S. Marine Corps just a few days after I turned eighteen. I was so tired of life; and all that I thought it was. I thought the marines would square me away, wrong. I knew life was not simple, but it just kept on getting harder to understand for me.

"The secret of success is consistency of purpose," is what Benjamin Disraeli once said. (In case you do not know who he was, Disraeli was born in London in 1839, and later became the Earl of Beaconfield. He was a brilliant debater and England's first and only Jewish prime minister, as well as well-known novelist). First, you have to have a purpose in life and I had not one idea what mine was. As I came to understand the Bible, I started to understand life. As soon as God told me what my purpose for being here was, I found peace, hope, and joy of living to give. It was amazing.

The first course on my list to study and listen to on tape was The Bible: FACT OR FICTION? By Dr. Robert G. Witty. What a great book for all of those who have any doubt about the Bible's authenticity. I strongly suggest it to a few of my siblings and the rest of you who doubt. You cannot help but see that, with the facts, there is no other way to live than to by the Bible's words. I love it. However, I am getting off track here.

What I wanted to tell you is that we cannot sleep on the job while we are here on earth: so little time and so much to tell, at least for me. We all must have a purpose in life, don't we? You do not, you say. Then, may I suggest this: ask Him what it is. Stop sleeping. Wake up and start reading. Awaken to a new day with one goal in your life, to know what your purpose is here on earth. I know once you find that out, it will be the happiest, most exciting day and the most heartfelt feeling of love that you will ever know for the rest of your life. Imagine that: the best. How exciting can life get that is more exciting than that? Nothing comes close to it.

I know that if I wanted to, I could be a minister, right now. However, God has told me that it is too soon. As much as I want to do what it is that I wish I could do, I cannot. I know that once I am allowed to, I will again hit a new high in life. I can hardly wait, but alas, I must. Therefore, in the meantime, I plan to stay awake as long as I can and study. What a joy it is to know that each day I will learn something new to pass onto someone who may need to hear what it is I learned. By doing this, I will be allowed to help those less fortunate to be able to go to a library to order books, or to have someone close by to learn from. These people will be the very people God has told me I will be helping. They are the young, the old, the homeless, and the veterans. To Him, I say thank you, thank you, and thank you.

Seeing how I am so wide-awake now, I think I'll go outside and spread a little joy.

I love you, but I could never love you as much as He does.

Brother Bob

What Does Satan Have To Do With It?

Aloha family, friends and all of God's children,

The year was 1995. February is a wonderful time of year in Hawaii. Every day in Hawaii is wonderful, but this year, something was about to happen that I would not forget for the rest of my life. It was the year of change, change beyond what no man on earth could possibly envision nor endure had he not the love of Jesus and our Father in Heaven living with in the heart.

I have survived many, many changes and challenges throughout my life thus far. I pray that no one has to go through life with even one of these miserable things coming across their path. I am well aware that some have suffered much more. That I should look upon my heartache as something any less miserable than theirs would be foolish on my part. There are many kinds of suffering. It just depends on who it is and what it is that they are going through. Some take hardship and pain well (meaning they are stronger than others) and others get to the brink of suicide. However, no matter who you are, Satan is the one who is behind it all.

Satan (I even hate to have to capitalize his name here) is very much a part of this world we live in. I know this because I have gone to war with him and his demons. If someone were to tell me what I am about to tell you right now I would think him or her a very insane person. If I did not know the Lord as my personal savior, I surely would not have endured the fight and the control of my mind as a human. God, Satan, and I went to war and God won. I wish to tell this story for the nonbelievers of the world. Everything is true to the best of my memory. I would pray that I never lie, but to say in any way that I am perfect would be a lie. However, I am not lying. The Lord would surely punish me if I were to do such a thing on purpose. Please keep an open mind as we go along; things will get strange. Actually, the things were strange, evil, and beyond man's thinking.

Satan comes to steal, kill, and destroy. I had been sober for two days. I had been drinking for four years straight. I was homeless for four years (Homeless for thirteen years in total, but that's another story.) and living in a park here in Honolulu, Hawaii. The name of the park was Thomas Square, a very green, clean and tree-filled park. It had a fountain in the center of it, and every six minutes, it would spray fifteen feet high. People from the community would come to show off their dogs or their children each day. On weekends, there would be craft shows or some type of entertainment. In the evening, it was quiet but for the drunks, such as me. Gay men would meet in the dark roots of the huge banyans. (Banyan trees have their roots growing down, instead of up from the ground, so there are plenty of roots to hide between.) The other drunks and the druggies would sit around talking like fools and trying to stay out of fights, or start one.

Living in this park was not an easy task when everyone is out of control after a couple of hours or so. However, for the last two days, I stayed to myself. I did not want to be around these people when I was sober. No one who comes into the park wants to be around us either. As I was sitting and thinking about how I could have gotten myself so deep into self and not trying to do something about it, I begin to get angry with Satan. I blamed Satan for all of my problems.

I thought to myself, "Bob, God spoke to you audibly in 1990. He told you of many things that were to come and some have come true, others you are waiting for to happen. But since He spoke to you, why is that you blame Satan when you know it is your fault"?

Things like that were going in and out of my mind for hours. Finally, I said, "Satan, I challenge you to a fight, you, me, and God. I know you're tough and you can do many things to me, but I believe that by my faith in God, and with Jesus at my side, you haven't a chance." I did not know at that time that I was never to challenge Satan. What was I to do? Satan had been pushing me for four years. It was four years ago that God had told me I would one day travel to many nations and speak to thousands and thousands of people. God had told me that I would feel great sorrow and soon after, I did, when one of my brothers died. He told me many other things including the part when He said

I would have four more years of pain and sorrow. (I did not know it at the time I challenged Satan but this was the almost the beginning of the fifthyear. I also didn't know at the time that just before God is ready to do something very big in your life, Satan comes to steal, kill, and destroy.)

It is evening now and I am sitting on the bench looking up into the star-filled night sky. (Before I go any further here, I would like to tell you that even though you may be an alcoholic and a sinner, you can still believe in the Lord and in God, our Father. I know I did. There are people all over the world who go to church every Sunday but sin all week; ask them. However, like me, they are saved sinners. If you are saved as well, then you know what I am talking about.) I am sitting there and I feel the Holy Spirit all around me: God was in the sky, in the park, in my heart, and in my soul. I was feeling so blessed to know Him. Just as I thought I could not feel any higher, I heard a voice. This voice said to me, "You will go to the Big Island and you will bomb two buildings." I thought to myself, "Could this be God?" I was truly bewildered. I said to myself aloud, "Why would I want to go to the Big Island and bomb some buildings?" I thought that if this were God, why would He want me to do such a thing. "But who else could it be?" I thought. Then I started to laugh aloud, and I said, "I know it's you, Satan. You think that you can fool me? I have to admit you stopped me in my tracks there, boy. I say to you this: Satan, be gone in the name of the Lord Jesus Christ. Get thee behind me." I said these things because they were the only things that I could remember from church or in the Bible, that I felt would get him out of my hair.

After telling Satan to hit the road, I went to the place where I had been sleeping for the last month and a half. There is a church right across from the park. It is a bit chilly in January in Honolulu and I had but one blanket. As I made myself as comfortable as possible on the cold cement, I felt as though someone was watching. We have all felt that feeling now and then. It was as if I knew someone was there, but yet it was not real, and yet, it was. I tried to dismiss it and block it out of my mind. However, I could not. I said, "Is that you, Satan?" No answer. I said, "I know it's you because if it were God, I would have peace and calmness. You must think I'm scared about now don't you? Listen, you're starting to piss me off." That's what I said, but inside I was scared. In fact, I was really scared. As I lay there, I kept my eyes closed because I was too scared to keep them open. I was afraid that if I opened them, I would see something I did not want to. That is not possible to do, however, when you are a fighter. I wanted to survive this war, so I opened my eyes. I wish that I had not the minute I saw them.

Satan has his demons and people who live in the secular world have theirs. I wish that I had not challenged Satan the minute I saw them. There were about eight or nine of these heads floating above me. They had all different kinds of colors. They did not have round heads like us. They had little spike like things coming out all around the top and sides of them. It was strange because I didn't know why they had no bodies. I started to pray hard then. I said, "Father, I'm so sorry for doing this. I pray that you step up and stop this, Lord. I can't take this, Father." I was scared and Satan knew it. I covered my head praying repeatedly to God. "What the heck did I get into now?" I thought. Those demons kept talking and yelling all night. It was a night in hell. I pray with all my heart that no one ever has to go through a night such as that.

By morning, I was a wreck. "I must look pretty bad after all that," I thought. When I walked over to the park, it was 4:30 in the morning. Satan kept on talking to me. Strange things like, "You're not a bad guy, Bob," and "Why don't you listen to me when I talk to you? You're my friend, Bob." Things that would make me think he was good and I would be happy if I listened to him. It was scary because I felt there was nothing I could do. I would just keep asking God for help, but I was not getting it. "God isn't with me", I thought to myself. How was that possible? Why would he let me go through this? Question after question was going around and around in my head all night and now into the day. As it became light, I saw my best friend, Ricko.

Ricko was a vet of two wars. Ricko had been a marine as well as a navy man. I met Ricko four years earlier, when I first came to sleep in the park. Bothof us being veterans, we became friends very quickly. I was a Vietnam vet, so Ricko had a lot of respect for me. Although I was nine years older than he was, I showed him the same respect he gave me. Ricko took one look at me, and said, "Bob, you look like you been up all night, brother." I then told him what had been going on. The thing about Ricko is that he always believed me. He knew that if I told him something, it was true (at least in my mind, it was). Ricko believes in God and he believes there is a Satan, as well. After all, how can you believe in the Lord and not believe what He has taught you about Satan. I could tell by the look on his face that he was concerned about me. I wanted to make some jokes about the whole thing, but for the first time in my life, I did not want to try to joke my way out of this. This was too big to be playing games and Satan kept on talking. The rest of the day, Ricko kept an eye on me. I must have seemed like I was going mad. I didn't eat anything all day. This was not anything new for me because I would normally fill up on booze. I was becoming weak, so I spent most of the day lying down beside the stone wall out of sight of the people coming in and out of the area.

It was becoming night time again, and I knew it was going to be a long one. I walked over to the place where I normally slept and found that someone else beat me to it. Therefore, I went to the front of the church and tried to sleep under some trees, under the cover of a twofoot overhang. It was worse this night with the demons and the voices, and it started to rain as well. I decided to walk over to the Honolulu Art Academy and try to stay dry, where homeless people are not to sleep, in the front entrance. No police showed up and I was somewhat disappointed because at that time, jail sounded like a safe place. The night was long. I was beat; Satan was having a time of his life tormenting me with his voice and his little buddies, as I began to call them. One time, I said, "Hey Satan, why don't you and I and your little buddies go and get messed up?" It was a joke but Satan took me seriously.

He said, "You can do that after we get to the Big Island." He was sure determined to get me to go to the Big Island. Then he and his demons started all over again to torment me.

It was morning now, (the night was sleepless) about 3:00 a.m. or so, and I would have to wait for another two hours before Ricko showed up. I wanted badly to see a friend so I had someone to talk to besides these demons in my head. I began to start believing that I was supposed to go to the Big Island. Why? Where was I to get material to make a bomb? Where was I to get the money? Satan told me to get the money from the church, "Maybe it really is God I am talking to and not Satan", I thought. I was tired and starting to get delirious.

I decided to go to the bathroom and try to clean up the best I could. I then went to the park to wait for my church, Word of Life, to open.

Ricko came into the park about 6:00 a.m. and I told him my plan to go to the church and ask for money. He asked if I was going to tell them the truth and I said, "Only as much as it will take to get the money." As I began to walk to the church, one of my brothers (I have six brothers and five sisters, nine still living and three with the Lord), who lives near the park, happened to be driving by. He stopped his car and asked if I needed a ride anywhere. I told him I was going to my church to ask for help on a certain matter and he said he had the time to take me there. Once we came close to the church, he asked me if I wanted him to wait so he could drive me back to the park. I said it was up to him and I was not sure how long it would take. He said he would wait as I walked into the office of Word of Life.

This was not the first time that I have asked a church for money. I did it two others times. Once I asked for $20.00 for gas in NorthDakota and once in southern California, for food money. It did not feel right somehow asking God's children for money that they could use for other things to help the church. "That can't be bothering me now," I thought to myself as I walked up to the receptionist at her desk. "I would like to talk to someone about helping me get a ticket to the Big Island," I said.

She asked me to wait a moment and she soon came back. She guided me to the head of the treasury department — or something like that — and asked me to have a seat. "Oh good, it's time to beg," I thought as I tried to humor myself through this insane situation.

"How can I help you, Bob?" she said.

I thought, "Wow, God told her I was coming."

She was surprised at me for laughing to myself. She said with a smile, "Did I miss something?'

"No, no, I was just thinking about something. Do I know you?"

Now she laughed and she told me her name and that we had spoken to one another many times before. I told her how sorry I was for not remembering her and I began to tell her I had to get to the Big Island. I told her that I was not sure why I was to go to the Big Island, but I did know that God was involved and I was sure I was supposed to go. She said that they do not give out money unless it is an emergency, and even then, they could only do it if it did not hurt their finances. She said that right now they could not help me.

"Where is God when you need Him?" I said to myself, to ease the confusion I was feeling.

I thanked the church for their time and I left thinking I had left a good impression of myself, but I found out later that I did not. (About three months after that visit to the church, I was told (by my now wife) that they said I was acting very strange, and they did not know if I was drunk or crazy. If I had told them all that was happening to me, they would have given me a ride to the airport, bought me the ticket, and thanked the Lord for allowing them to help protect their church from what they thought was a madman.)

Once I was outside, I saw that my brother was still waiting, and I jumped into his car. He asked how it went and I told him that they did not have the funds to give. Bill then asked me why I needed the money. I said, as I was smiling, "I know you won't believe this, but Satan and I are having a war. The good news is that I have God and Jesus on my side, so I'll be okay. Satan has been talking to me for the last two nights with his little demons so I haven't slept for two nights now."

Bill looked at me with his eyes wide open and said, "Man, you've really lost it this time haven't you?"

I started to laugh very hard and when I stopped, I said, "I expected that from you, Bill, but it's true. You know, I don't joke about this kind of thing."

Bill said, "Yup, you're totally out of it."

I laughed some more, and by this time, we were near the park. I said, "I'm not losing it and I'm not nuts, Bill, this is for-real stuff." As I closed the door, Bill was sitting there shaking his head, and I think he was shocked to hear what I had just told him.

Since that time I left Bill sitting there wide-eyed and bewildered, I have learned so much. One thing I have learned is this: "A prophet is not with out honor except in his own country, among his relatives, and in his own house" (Mark 6:4). That is to say, my siblings will not know me if they know not the Lord. They shall think my ways foolish and my words as lost as my mind. However, I shall continue to pray for them each day forward in the name of my Father and hope that one day they shall answer the door when He knocks. (I love it when the Holy Spirit steps in and takes over my words.)

I decided I would go to Tripler Hospital to see if I could get some sleep. After arriving and waiting for an hour or so, a doctor came to ask me questions. I did not know how else to tell him what was wrong with me so I told him the truth. After I finished telling him that Satan and I were at war, he acted as if he knew just what to do. I thought to myself that four or five men would be showing up at any time to put a straightjacket on me. As I was waiting, I happened to peek out of the curtains. I saw my doctor standing over to the side talking to three other doctors. Just as they were talking, my doctor looked over at my bed and they all turned to look. It seemed to me that they looked like they had just heard something very different in the medical field . I sat back and waited for the boys to come with the wrap around jacket. However, to my surprise, the doctor came back in and said that all I needed was some rest. I said, "I told you that, but you haven't given me an answer as to how I'm to go about that with Satan around."

Just then, Satan said to me, "They're not going to help you. No one can help you but me. Relax and everything will be fine."

It sounded to me like he was under the bed so I said to the doctor,

"Do you hear him? He is right there under the bed. Didn't you hear him?"

"He won't do anything, Bob," said Satan.

The doctor must have been nervous by now. Nevertheless, I was getting a little angry that they would not help and I said to the doctor, "There's nothing you can give me to make me sleep?"

He said, "Mr. Dunham, please just go home and lay down and you'll soon be asleep."

Satan was right: I was going to get nowhere with these people. I walked out and chewed out Satan all the way to the park.

As I walked back into the park, I saw all the men hanging around, getting drunk and starting their day out trying to figure out how they could drink all day. I did not want to talk to anyone, so I went to lie in a corner of two park walls. I lay their all day fighting my demons and praying that this would all soon end in the name of Jesus. About 2:00 p.m., another friend came to me and told me he had my SSI (Social Security Income) check. Now, I am getting even more confused. Did God send this check at this time, at this hour, to go to the Big Island, or was I going mad? I prayed to God to give me direction as to what to do with the check. I felt that He wanted me to wait a little longer for His answer. I did not agree with Him but I knew I would have to wait.

It started to become dark, and Ricko came to me and said with a slight laugh, "Brother, I don't ask of much from you, do I?"

I told him no, but I expected him to ask something of me now, because of the tone of his voice.

His laugh became a little uncomfortable and he said, "Brother, I want you to let me call an ambulance."

I told him that that would not be necessary. He then said with tears in his eyes, "Bob, you're going to die if you don't let me call them; I can feel it in my heart. I love you, brother, and I don't want you to die."

"Maybe he's right," I thought to myself. "If I went into the emergency ward, they would take care of me."

(I found out later in time that I had had another seizure that night. I had them often when I didn't sleep or eat. Ricko did not tell me I had one that night, for whatever reason he might have had.)

Soon, the ambulance came. The last thing I remembered after they put me in the ambulance was waking up to the phone ringing next to my hospital bed. It was Ruth (my future wife) and she said that my brother, Jerry, who lived on the Big Island, had a minor stroke. He wanted to know if I wanted to come over and help him and to try to get myself sober again. I told her I would pray about it and hung up. "What kind of a twist was this?" I thought. Now, I am thinking, "Is this God or Satan?" Therefore, I asked God if He wanted me to go to the Big Island, and as I was praying, I fell back asleep.

I was in and out of sleep all day. I could not tell you what they did to me or who I spoke to. However, I will never forget the next morning: I awakened, with the phone ringing. This time, after I said hello, I heard another familiar voice. It was my brother, Jerry, on the Big Island. All he said was, "Are you coming or not?"

I have no idea why I said it; it just came out in an instant, "Yup. I'll be on the next flight." I hung the phone up and started to pull the IVs out of my arm. A nurse saw me and ran to get the doctor and some others to stop me.

When the doctor came in, he told me that if I left with out their permission, that I would probably come back in a body bag next time. He had taken care of me on many occasions for my alcohol problem.

I had stayed in Tripler for three months at a time, four different times. This doctor knew I was about at the end of the line.

I said, "Doc, I don't know why I'm doing this. I only know that this is what the Lord wants me to do." I knew in my heart, in every way possible, that God wanted me to leave at this very moment. Therefore, I dressed and headed out for the airport.

As I walked out of the hospital, I felt, at that very moment, that things in my life were about to change dramatically. I knew, inside, that I would never have a drink again. I also knew that the war with Satan had ended. I looked up into the sky and stretched out my arms. I said, "Thank you, Father, thank you, thank you, thank you." I was in such a wonderful state of mind that I could not possibly describe it. I told the Lord that I knew that what I was going to the Big Island for was not to set off a bomb, but to help a brother in need. I told Him how grateful I was for Him helping me to fight Satan. I told Him how sorry I was for even doing such a stupid thing as asking Satan to battle in the first place. I told Him repeatedly that I did not doubt Him, but I did have doubts at times, if I was going to make it all the way. (I know, that I know, that I know, He already knew that.)

I had to get to the point of no return before I could return to His pathway, on His terms, and by His Grace. As I mentioned earlier, I was told by Him that I had to go through four years of pain and sorrow. After I had arrived onto the Big Island, I realized and I relished the fact that it was now the beginning the fifthyear since God had spoken to me. The things that happened and the changes in my life, at the point when I walked out of the hospital, have been indescribable. I have many, many wonderful stories of what happened after I reached the Big Island. However, that's "the rest of the story." God always keeps His word.

I was an alcoholic and drug user, a womanizer, a con, a thief, and a liar, and I had little integrity. God answered my prayers by talking to me audibly. What He has told me has come true or is in His works. I have nothing to gain by telling anyone this story. On the other hand, if you see what Satan tried to do to me, if you take this story seriously, then you have everything to gain if you ask God to come into your life. Do something for yourself and others by asking Him for help. It does not matter to me if you stay the way you are. I do not know you, but I feel for you because you have no idea what you are missing. Start a new life living as God would have you live.

> *"Is there any one among you who is wise and understanding? He is to prove it by his good life, by his good deeds performed with humility and wisdom. But if in your heart, you are jealous, bitter, and selfish, don't sin against the truth by boasting of your wisdom. Such wisdom does not come down from heaven; it belongs to the world, it is unspiritual and demonic. Where there is jealousy and selfishness, there is also disorder and every kind of evil.*
>
> *"But the wisdom from above is pure first of all; it is also peaceful, gentle, and friendly; it is full of compassion and produces a harvest of good deeds; it is free from prejudice and hypocrisy. And goodness is the harvest that is produced from the seeds the peacemakers plant in peace."*
>
> *-James 3:13-18*

"The Lord was with me when Satan came,
The Lord protected me and new strength I did gain."

"Lord, I pray with all my heart that, as a child of God, I do good deeds with humility and wisdom. I pray that I have a harvest of good deeds that are full of compassion, that I will be peaceful, gentle, and friendly, free from prejudice and hypocrisy. I pray as a peacemaker that goodness is the harvest of the seeds. In Jesus's name I pray, Amen."

Much Mahalo for letting me share. God bless you always and forever.

"I love you, but I can never love you as much as He does."

Brother Bob
A grateful child of God

One of God's Children

Aloha family, friends, and all of God's Children,

I received a call at 4:00 this morning, from my wife in Minnesota. Because of the hour of the day, I knew it would be her.

Sometimes, it is hard to walk through life by faith alone. However, it is possible. I was waiting for this call for a few days, for I knew what was coming.

"Hello," I said.

"Hi, honey." My wife said, with a choked voice. I could vision the tears in her eyes, and her sorrow flowed through my body and my heart.

"The doctor called the family about Peggy. She has not much time. I had so much faith in Jesus to heal her, Bob," Ruth said.

I said, "I know, honey, but you have to remember that we live by faith and we will die with faith. God has control over everything, honey." She then asked me to pray for the family and she would call to keep me informed.

I really did not know what to say. Even though I had seen this coming for several days, I still was not prepared for it. Peggy (Ruth's sister and fifty-four years young) just went to the doctor to find out why she had a pain in her side last week. After x-rays, they told her she had cancer. Now, nine days later, to hear my wife say Peggy is going home to be with our Father is quite a shock. We never expected that, nor would we even think it. After Ruth and I said goodbye, I went to the Bible and turned on the TV for the morning services they have each Sunday.

"For we walk in faith and not by sight" (2 Corinthians 5:7). That is what I was led to read in the Bible. At the same time on the TV, I heard Doctor Robert Schuller say, "She will be in eternal light and life forever more."

Do you see how God speaks through us at our time of need? God was telling me that Peggy was going to be in His arms soon and that she will always be in that eternal light. God is amazing to me. When you are a child of God and the Holy Spirit lives with in, He speaks to us to soothe and comfort us. I knew Peggy for only eight years but I felt that I knew her better than I knew my older sister, Pat, who went to be with the Lord in 1997. She, too, passed away with cancer. However, Pat was twelve years older than I was so I hardly ever saw her. In addition, when Pat and I lived in the same city, Seattle, Washington, I still did not see her because I was the prodigal son.

I saw Peggy less than Pat over my life time; however, I saw and spoke more openly and honestly with Peggy. We became very close friends in a short period. She told me things that she said she had told no one but her sister Carolyn. Carolyn and Peggy were like Siamese twins. If you saw one walking down the street, you saw the other as well. I never saw any two people who were closer, other than my brother George and me. One of the things that I would like to share with you is Peggy's heart. She had a huge one. She loved people and always found something good about everyone she met. One of the things we used to joke about was our age difference, as I am one day older. She used to joke about me being her "big brother." It was a real joy laughing with her when we had the blessing of seeing one another. I will miss that, as well as much more. She will be missed dearly until we meet again.

We are God's sheep. We are His flock, His children. I would think that when you leave this earth, you want to be where He is. It is impossible for me to tell you all the reasons you should give your life to our Father, but there is one thing you can do to help yourself. Open the Bible and read what it says. One of the major mistakes I made in life was not taking the time to see what Christians were talking about, because if I had, it would have changed my life sooner. All I had to do was to open the Bible. Even though being a disbeliever, I still could have investigated the matter for myself, to see what the truth was. Boy, I was stupid. However, hey, it's never too late to learn, I found out. It is at times like these that I am truly grateful to God for His forgiving me of my foolishness. I am blessed and you will be as well, if you care to ask for His help.

When the Lord told me to start my non-profit outreach program, I had no idea what to call it. He told me to call it, "Songs of the Children, for the Children." Many of you know how much we were able to help others in need on the Big Island of Hawaii. However, what I want to tell you is this, "Today, I will sing a song for a child of God." In fact, I will sing many songs today for this child of God. I will give God the Glory for not letting Peggy go through countless hours of pain and suffering. I will sing of His love for Peggy and for His gracing us to have had Peggy in our lives. I will sing long and feel proud of Peggy's love for our Father with whom she has gone home. There shall be, "Songs of the Children," in the church soon to give glory to our Father and to Peggy. Praise God and our Lord Jesus Christ. "God's Children, singing songs of praise for His Child Peggy to His Children in the Church." ("Songs of the Children, for the Children.") There are not enough words to express my love for you Peggy. I will end this letter the way I ended all of my letters to you:

"I love you, but I could not love you as much as He does."

Your Brother in the Lord, Bob

From the Heart

Aloha, family, friends, and all of God's children,

As we walk, glide, fly, or whatever other way you wish to picture your time travel here on earth, you cannot help but have to think about if there is a God or not. Thus far, I have been writing things from the heart and from the soul of my life. However, today, when I was watching Joyce Meyer, I had thoughts of homelessness and of love. I want to help these people so badly. However, can I? I asked God and suddenly I started to sing a song from the past. (He always brings to me the oldies but goodies.) The words that went repeatedly in my mind were, "I love how you love me, I love how you love me, I love how you squeeze me, feed me, and need me, I love how you love me."

I know those are not the exact words to that song from long ago, but I do remember the song. It reminded me of when I had started to buy all of these old songs in Kailua-Kona on the Big Island. I had about four hundred dollars worthof tapes before someone stole them out of my car. All the oldies that I had planned to have the band play and the group sing once we had formed our, "Songs of the Children," band. Oh yes, it is still going to happen, but I just do not know when.

It is what was put in my heart. I want to be like Paul and go out in the bush, go from town to town, and from homeless dwelling to homeless dwelling, and spread God's word. I want to go into some open field and have food for those who are hungry and feed them while the band is singing words of hope and bring joy to those who are lost. It is impossible for me to explain to you how I feel when I get these feelings. If you knew the Lord, you would understand. However, I feel so good inside, as if I am lifted up inside. Boy, it is hard to explain.

On page 15 of The Bible: Truth or Fiction written by Dr. Robert G. Witty it says, "The personal testimony —a gift from God whose value cannot be estimated — remains a claim based only on a subjective experience. What the Christian can declare, the skeptic can deny or attribute to a natural cause. And if what the Christian testifies about the deity source of his salvation falls short of proving its validity of the Bible based upon a subjective experience will likewise fall short of objective proof to the skeptic." What Dr. Witty is saying is that the skeptic will always need more proof. Therefore, I suggest that you read Dr. Witty's book for the proof of the Bible's word.

Again, I am getting off base here. I want to tell you that if we have the heart of God, we can do anything. "From the heart," comes from God. (With God in your heart, you have a pot of gold.) It is a wonderful, wonderful feeling when He comes to me with songs such as this morning. If you want to have a song in your heart that is like no other song, even if you have heard the song fifty times, then you should hear how He sings it. From His heart to yours is the point I am making. It is glorious indeed. Although I have had the Holy Sprit come over me many, many times, I still cannot believe the miracle of it all. I love our Father in Heaven so much; I cannot put it in words. How I wish that I could just wave a wand and let you feel what I feel. I cannot, but you can ask Him how it feels if you like.

"I love you, but I could never love you as much as He does."

Brother Bob

Mmmmm...Do I Look This Harsh?

Aloha family, friends and all of God's children,

Are you harsh, hard, sharp, and pressing?

Would you not rather be wholesome, useful, good, comfortable, gracious, and pleasant?

You could be gentle (meek) and humble (lowly) in heart. In addition, find rest (relief, ease, refreshment, recreation and blessed quiet) for your soul.

The definition of the word "meekness" from Vine's Greek dictionary (the gist of it, at least) is that meekness is Christ's own gentle and soothing disposition and is an "inwrought grace of the soul."

Getting rid of a hard heart is not easy. However, maybe, if you carry around in your wallet or handbag, this definition of the word, meekness, and try to change your way of thinking to think as Jesus did, you, too, can be meek. For the "meek" shall inherit the earth, saiththe Lord.

Please read, in the Amplified Bible, Matthew 11:29-30.

"I love you, but I could never love you as much as He does."

Brother Bob

Joyce Meyer Ministries, Letter Two

Joyce Meyer Ministries
P.O. BOX 655 · FENTON, MO 63026 · (636)349-0303
www.joycemeyer.org

December 23, 2003

Robert Dunham
P.O. BOX 8967
Honolulu, Hawaii 96830-0967

Dear Robert,

We want to thank you for inviting us to meet with you. However, due to our very busy schedule, we will not be able to accommodate your request. In your letter, you had also asked how my brother, David, is doing. We appreciate your concern.

At this time, David has left the St. Louis area. We are not sure where he is or what he is doing. However, we believe in God's faithfulness to His Word in Philippians 1:6, "...convinced and sure of this very thing, that He Who began a good work in (David) will continue until the day of Jesus Christ...,"

Thank you for caring enough to write. We ask that you keep David in your prayers. May the Lord bless you in all that you do.

In God's love,

Dave and Joyce Meyer

I Am So Confused

Dear Joyce, a mentor and my sister in our Lord Jesus Christ,

Aloha,

Thank you, from my heart, for taking the time to reply to my letter. In addition, I give the glory to God.

It saddens me to hear that your brother, Dave, has moved on. I agree whole-heartedly with you when you quoted the scripture Philippians 1:6. Knowing what I, myself, have experienced with alcohol and then giving my life to the Lord, only to be homeless for another four years, I truly believe that God will continue His good works until the day of Jesus Christ. Just as I had told Iverna Tompkins in the letter that I sent her (a copy of which I sent to you) in which I had told of my trials with Satan and how God changed everything when I left the hospital. I, too, had to confront what needed to be confronted. David will also, I believe. I found in life that people often do things, and others have no idea why they do them. Everyone knows this but do any of them take the time to listen to that person everyone is trying to figure out? (Not many.) They may listen, but do they hear? One day, David will find out that the best ear that he has, that not only listens but also hears, is God's. I envy you for when that day comes, and it will, because David will do just as I did when I found the Lord with in me, he will come to you to share that joy. My older sister, God rest her soul, was a Christian for forty-five years before she left to go home. She once told me that she prayed for me, every day, which I would one day give my life to God. When I did, I could not wait to get on the phone and tell her "the good news."

When, Patricia (Pat) left us, I went to Seattle to be at the service to give my regards to the family. At the service, the congregation was asked if anyone wished to speak. I had already prepared a letter, which I had hoped I would be able to share with everyone if given the opportunity. I mentioned first that two of my brothers, who could not be there, asked me to give their condolences for them. I then told them about how Pat had prayed for all of her brothers and sisters to one day know the Lord as their personal savior. It was important enough to her so much so that she prayed on her knees daily for this.

I then told the church how I was the prodigal son and one of the brothers that she had prayed the hardest for to receive the Lord in my heart. I told them how after I had accepted Jesus Christ as my personal savior, she began to cry. I told them how she grabbed me by the hand and said, "Thank you, God," as she looked me in the eyes. Then she hugged me with the warmest embrace and told me how happy she was for me and how much she loved me.

Then the church began to say, "Praise God, Praise God".

That church was a very big church, Joyce, and was filled into the balcony. People had to stand in the back of the church and outside to be part of that service. Many loved her and more than that were there that day will miss her. My sister and you are much alike, Joyce, just as David and I are much alike. Your prayers to will be answered and so will David's, just as my sister's and mine were. God is so good.

I started this letter to thank you and speak of Dave. I also was going to ask you a question. However, as I was writing this letter, the Lord gave me what I believe to be the answer to my question. It is so wonderful that He gave me the answer and has made me so happy that I must share it with you.

The reason for the picture up on the top is that I had a question that was confusing me deeply. (Thus, the title, "I'm so confused." The picture went to the extreme just for a little levity ;-)

The question was this: How does one know what his or her gift is? It says in James 4:10, "As each one has received a gift, minister it to one another, as good stewards of the manifold grace of God." I had written a rough draft of what I wanted to say to you in a previous letter. I had many ideas in it about my thoughts on that question.

Then, I prayed to God before I started to write this letter. I asked Him to let me know what my gift is so I would not have to bother you and take up your time. Four hours later, I started to write and God revealed to me (by way of remembrance) that I had the gift of listening and hearing. Not only that, but that people trusted in me so much so that they would convey their innermost thoughts and feel comfortable doing so. They knew me to be "for real." This took me aback, at first, but as I thought about what he had told me, I knew that everything makes sense to me now. I believe that one of the reasons that He had me so involved with reading your books and listening to your tapes and watching your television show two or three times a day is because He knows that you, too, are "for real."

I was so happy to once again feel the grace of God fill my body, mind, and spirit. (Don't you just love that warm and loving feeling, Joyce? ; -) God is so wonderful; I think that you and I have had buckets full of tears from pain and suffering of the heart. Nevertheless, the bucket of tears, of joy, and love for our Father, far outweighs any other bucket of tears.

There you have it: the end. Just kidding, it is just the beginning. Each day that we have is a new day in our life, Joyce, and that truly excites me. Just to know God has something for us to hear, smell, see, share…and the list goes on and on. We are truly blessed, my sister, "one day at a time."

There is one other "big" thing I would like to ask you, Joyce: Could you pray and ask God, our Father, if there is anywhere in your ministry that you could use me? As I had said in one of the letters, I sent to you, the Lord told me I would be traveling from nation to nation speaking to thousands and thousands of people. It sure seems to me that we are like brother and sister. I know we are in the Lord and I pray you do not misunderstand me. However, it is as if I have known you for years. Maybe it is because you remind me of my real sister; I do not know. However, I do know that we are on the same path. I could quote scripture to everything that I say to try and make myself look like I know the Word inside out, but then I would be as a false witness. God would never allow me to do that. I would not want to appear anything that I am not. However, I am a child of God and if you should need me in any way of service please feel free to call upon me. Much Mahalo, for that.

I had better go. My wife, Ruth, gives you her love and tells me to say thank you as well for all that you have helped us with to know God and Jesus better. I always end my letters with the following,

"We love you Joyce, but we could never love you as much as He does."

(After thought, It should not be, "God be with you," it should be "God is with you, always.")

"Once you open the door when He knocks, your life is filled with light, and He will answer those things that confuse you."

Brother Bob

This Is My Gift to You

Aloha, family, friends and all of God's children,

When watching Joyce Meyer this morning, she was on the subject of giving. I took some time after the show to think about the best gift I had received, and to whom and what the best gift I have ever given was.

I think but seconds, I know that the greatest gift in my life — and until I am called home to be with our Father — was the forgiveness of my sins. However, to recall what gift I myself have given and to whom, had taken some time, indeed. I did not want to think of the "best gift" as being something material. Anyone can give a watch, a ring, or a bouquet of flowers. However, what had I given to someone that means something to him or her as much today, as the day I gave it to them? Mmmmm...

I gave a friend of mine a puppy when I was small. He really liked it but I am sure he does not have it today. Mmmmm...I could say that when I saved a man's life from drowning in the river in Washington was the best. However, that was not really a gift from me — that was from God. Mmmmm....let's see. I gave my wife a wedding ring, but hey, that goes with the territory. (Right, honey? ;-)

I wish I could say that I gave my mother the happiest gift she had when I quit drinking, but again, that was God. When it comes right down to it, God always gives the best gifts. You know the old saying, "You can't out give God." Oh, some of you don't know that one, do you. Well, I hope you will one day. Anyway, where was I? Oh, yes, the best gift I gave.

Well, I hope this does not sound anything but humble, but I would say that being able to give my testimonial is the best gift I have given. I believe that sharing my love for the Lord and our Father in heaven is just about the best thing I have given or have to give, for that matter. Taking the time to share with others all that He has done for me is what makes me feel the best. God gave us the ability to love one another and give of ourselves. I hope that I take full advantage of His love to do so.

Next time you decide to give, please do not forget to tell them as well,

"I love you, but I could never love you as much as He does."

Aloha,
Brother Bob

A Grunt

10/9/03

Aloha family, friends and all of God's children,

When I was in the U.S. Marine Corps, I was a grunt. A grunt is someone who is actually a killing machine and a hard worker when it calls for getting a tough job done. (You grunt a lot when you work hard. Is that why they called us grunts. ;-) I have a brother who was in the Marine Corps, as well, and he said to me one day, "Are you always going to be a grunt"? The reason he said that was because at the time we were talking about hard, laborious tasks. I had been working hard on the building I manage and it occurred to him that I have not changed my work ethics.

At first, I laughed about his remark. However, after thinking about it for some time, I came to realize that, yes; I still am a "grunt." I am not the grunt I used to be. I did become "all that I could be" when I was in the Corps. Now that my life is in the Lord's hands, I have a new life to live; I am a soldier for God now. "I am all that He wants me to be".

You cannot be the same person you once were before you gave your life to the Lord. It is impossible to do. Once you ask the Lord to take over and the Holy Spirit comes in, you are not the same person anymore. You have started a new life, literally. I must stay a grunt if I am to fulfill what it is that our Father in Heaven calls me to do.

Paul was a grunt in every sense of the word. Peter, John, Mark, and Luke were all grunts. King David was a full-fledged grunt if ever there was one. David first took care of his father's flock of sheep, and in doing so; he had to kill a bear and a lion. Then he put big ole Goliathdown with a stone and cut his head off. David was not finished after that great win because he then went out to war and slew thousands of enemy soldiers.

The Bible is filled with grunts. I would like to think that "grunt" is just another way of calling me a "soldier of God." Unlike what is said on the TV, "Be all that you can be", I say, "I pray that I will be all that He calls me to be." I have no control of my life now; He does.

You, too, can choose to let the Lord guide you on His pathway if you so wish. I pray you do, because no man is a soldier who stands alone. A true soldier is guided by his love for the Lord, for there is no better love than this. In addition, a good soldier knows that he cannot help all those who need help when he goes it alone. What better way is there to win than if not by being led by our Father in heaven and walking with other children of God along the way?

There are many words in the Bible that I would like to quote scripture. However, the following are words I feel that makes it very clear why everyone should pick up the cross:

Matthew 16:24-28

Then Jesus said to His disciples, "If anyone desires to come after Me, let him deny himself, and take up his cross, and follow me. For whoever desires to save his life will lose it, but whoever loses his life for My sake will find it. For what profit is it to a man if he gains the whole world, and loses his own soul? Or what will a man give in exchange for his soul? For the Son of Man will come in the glory of His Father with His angels, and then He will reward each according to his works. Assuredly, I say to you, there are some standing here who shall not taste deathtill they see the Son of Man coming in His Kingdom."

"I love you, but I could never love you as much as He does".

Brother Bob

Certainty in Your Life

Dear family, friends, and all of God's children,

For a person to have certainty in his or her life, he or she must first understand what it means. "That's simple," you may think to yourself. However, is it really? Certainty is what you and I think of when we know for sure that we will wake up in the morning and think of what the day is going to bring. The key words here are "wake up."

If I were to ask you, "Are you sure you're going to wake up?" you would say, "Of course."

However, how can you be certain?

"A burglar could come into your home and take your life tonight," I might say, "Are you certain that if you were to die in your sleep tonight, you would go to where there is peace?"

"It doesn't matter," you would reply.

"It doesn't matter?"

Would it matter not, if you had a choice between peace and sorrow when you leave here? All of your life, you have been making choices and now for some reason you think, "It doesn't matter!" Our whole life is based on choices. Right or wrong choices; it does not matter! What if I were say to you, "I know of a choice you can make, that if you choose to, the choice you make could change the outcome of your life, bothhere and after you leave here?" Do you think you are wise enough to make the right choice? I know that if you make the right choice, you will never go through life again making your own decisions. On top of that, you will not want to make the choices anyway once you see you no longer must.

Think about what I have said. Then make the right choice and wait for God to do the rest.

I love you, but I could never love you as much as He does.

Brother Bob

No Need for a Troubled Mind

4/25/04

Aloha, my friends, family and all of God's children,

Back in the day (in my youth), I would worry every day about what would happen at school. Coming from a family of twelve children, my older brothers had left a bad impression with the teachers at our school. We grew up in a small town called New Rockford, in the state of NorthDakota. It was not a Mayberry in any sense of the word. Everyone knew who was who and how much trouble any child in the town caused. Therefore, when I started school, it was very clear to me by my first grade teacher that she did not like "the Dunham boys." She frightened me so badly that she made me wet my pants the very first day. However, that is another story in itself.

I went on into life with much fear, low self-esteem, and a whole lot of anger. I tried to cover it up by acting as if I was a tough guy. It was not until I went into the Marine Corps that I became even angrier and more insecure than I thought was possible.

My life of frustration with my inadequate life (that I felt at the time) led me to drink and get involved with drugs. After carrying those feelings around with me for forty-five years, I realized that I could never do what I wanted to do with out some help. I was tired of the fear and worry all the time. I was tired of not being able to help people the way I believed they needed help. To me, there was not enough compassion and love surrounding me.

Of course, my kind of lifestyle did not cater to those kinds of feelings. How could a drunk help people? How could selling drugs, getting into fights, moving in and out of jails, and using the "f" word in every other sentence, draw people of love and compassion into my life?

I believe that in the thirteen years that I was homeless; the loneliness was the most difficult part to bear with. I soon found out that worry was the best friend of loneliness. However, I was an adult now. How did all of this happen? Of course, you would not have to be a teacher out of New Rockford to know the answer to that. I needed help and I knew of a place to go that I had gone to before. Although I had no results from this place in the past, I felt that in some way it had to be the right place to try again. Some of you know where I went to, but for those of you who do not, I will tell you: I went to church.

I will not go any further on the subject of what happened. One day you will know about it. What I wish to tell you right now is that you can eliminate your worries about your problems this way: "Put your problems in the context of faith."

"Seek ye first the kingdom of God." His rule. He takes care of all our worries of problems, if you choose to let Him in. You and all of those you love, will have no worries if we all learn to live Christ like every day. Is there one reason why you and I should not wake up each morning and not think of God the very first thing? He is the guiding light. He is the ruler of our lives. What's so beautiful about this love is that He gives it unconditionally. He enjoys giving to us. When you wake up in the morning with Him on your mind, you will be joyful and you will want to know what He has in store for you for the day. It will not always be as pleasant as we wish nor as understandable as we would like it to be, but He is always there to see us through it all.

Next time you start to worry, put that worry in the context of your faith. Then go out to the garage and grab your fishing pole. Head on down toward the river and as you walk along, whistle a little tune. Be restful in your heart; God has control of everything.

I love you, but I could never love you as much as He does.

Brother Bob

Are You Pushing the Envelope?

Someone came to me long ago and said, "One day, I'm going to be somebody."

On a separate occasion, another person came to me and said, "I'm just a nobody and there's nothing I can do about it."

There was yet another who said, "I'm a 'want-a-be.'"

I said, "Just what do you think a, "want-a-be" is?"

He replied, "A person who wants to be this or be that, but never reaching his goal."

Do you want to be somebody? Are you a nobody? Are you a wanta-be? Are you pushing the envelope?

I was pushing the envelope for thirty-five years. When I first heard the term "pushing the envelope," I asked what it meant and my friend said that it meant that I was "going overboard or pressing too many buttons," or maybe, that I was pushing myself so hard that I was going to hurt someone just to reach my goals. I was only about thirteen or so when told this, but I never forgot those words. I have found in my fifty-three years of life here on earth that I was pushing buttons, going overboard, and hurting people. However, I was blind to most of it. I never took the time to understand what we are here on earth to do. I found out that "pushing the envelope" was just another way of saying that I was a selfish, arrogant, and ignorant person going through life doing things my way. What a silly, silly thing to do. You push the envelope as far as you can just to get your way. I suppose in some cases, it may have seemed necessary. However, in most cases, it is not. My belief was that we must think about our motives and intentions before we push the envelope. However, I did not do that. I just went fullsteam ahead and did whatever it took to get my way. I was pushing the envelope almost on a daily basis.

Today, however, I need not do such a thing. Now I just say, "Lord, I can't reach this goal with out your help. I give my toughest jobs to you because only you do what I cannot."

This eliminates the stress, the anger, the frustration, and all of the other sufferings we go through when we try to do everything our way instead of "letting go and letting God" guide us to accomplish His goals. I then have overwhelming peace and joy knowing that "whatever the outcome, it is meant to be so." In most cases, everything turns out great. Sometimes we have a hard time understanding the outcome. That is ok, too, because we still know "in our hearts" that in the result, God's way will be the right and only way.

As my friend and mentor always says, "Pray about everything."

"I love you, but I could never love you as much as He does".

Aloha, your Brother, Bob

God's Choices

Aloha, family, friends and all of God's children,

A man, who once lived before our time, was and will always be a part of my memory. Even though I knew him not personally, I feel in my heart that we share many ideals in the same manners of thought and affection in the heart. This man carried on his shoulders the weight of man and assigned to his duties as only God could have guided him.

This man walked as Jesus would have walked, as if Jesus surely was with in him. I believe that Jesus was a part of this man's spirit and soul. For the things that this man did reflected the acts that only Jesus himself would have accomplished had the shoes of said man been filled by Jesus himself.

If I could imitate a man, there would be two from which I would choose: the first would be Jesus Christ; the second would be that man who carried on his shoulders the weight of which only Jesus himself could understand and still hold up after being treated in the cruelest of ways. That man is Abraham Lincoln.

I am blessed to carry the sword of Jesus, and I pray that one day I may be blessed enough to be as wise and as strong as Abraham Lincoln. I will surely go home to my maker with honor. Knowing that I, too, was blessed by our Father to tell the world of my love of Him that saved me from my own destruction and gave to me a life filled with love for my fellow man.

Thank you, Father, for letting me see through thy own eyes and feel from my heart, the love that you have given unto me.

"I love you, but I could never love you as much as He does".

Brother Bob

This Is a Revival

Aloha family, friends and all of God's children,

I wanted to share something that I am sure will not happen again. I drove, as I do most mornings, down to Waikiki, listening to my music. The oldies but goodies always take me on a peaceful journey into days long ago forgotten but still in my heart. Today, I was driving along, listening to one of my most remembered tunes when I came to a stoplight. It was a very joyful morning. Then I looked to my right and saw a very beautiful woman who showed me her pearly whites. She made it clear that she was a man's street pleaser. I smiled back and said, "How's it?"

The light changed and I went on with my cruise. However, I could not put that smile out of my mind. I thought to myself, "I wonder what would happen if I went back and told her I would give her $20.00 to get her off her feet and take a cruise with me. I thought she could use a rest because she looked tired. It was 4:00 in the morning and surely, she could use a rest.

Therefore, after missing her on my first trip around a few blocks, I saw her at last standing near Starbucks. I had given this task at hand much thought while driving around looking for her. I thought to myself, "If I pick her up, she will think I'm a customer. So I have to make it very clear when I see her that I tell her just exactly what my intentions are."

I pulled up alongside of her and said, "Aloha, Sister. I thought maybe you could use a break and take a cruise around the block for a little rest."

She smiled as she reached for the door handle and bent in to look at me. She knew that she had seen me only minutes earlier as I was cruising down the street. She opened the door and sleeked her way into the seat.

She had on a very daring black dress with very little for the imagination to ignore, I noticed as I glanced quickly at her as she sat in the seat.

I told her, "I was just driving around enjoying my oldie but goodie tunes on the radio here and thought you could use a break."

She turned and smiled that eye-catching smile again and said to me, "Would you like to have some fun?"

I said, "I am having fun. This is what I do for fun sometimes. I listen to these sounds and it takes me to days of joy in my life."

She said, "Yeah, I know what you mean, but wouldn't you like to have fun with me?" She said this with a little touch of a pout. She said this in a way that I almost felt that if we did not have some kind of sex, I would hurt her little heart. She said it in a way that a little girl would ask for something very special and she needed it.

I had to laugh. I did not laugh out load but she noticed that I was smiling.

She said, "How much money do you have?" I told her that I had a few bucks but that I have never paid for sex before and had no intention doing so now.

"But don't you want to have me do something for you? I want to do something good for you." She said with a smile and that little pout. I had to laugh again because she was not going to give up easily. Just then, her little walkie-talkie went off and she answered it. It was another woman on the other line. I could hear it just as well as she could because it was on speaker. The other women asked where she was, and my rider said she was along Waikiki with someone. Her friend asked her if she could pick her up if she is in a car. My rider looked at me and I said, "Ask her where she is and we will go there." The woman on the other line said she was at the Hilton Village. She said she would be out front.

My rider asked if Zesty was with her and the person on the other end of the line replied that she was.

I told my rider that we were only a few blocks away and could be there in about three minutes.

After my rider hung up, she again asked me to help her out by letting her do something special for me. She said we could stop at an ATM and I could get $100.00 and she would take care of me.

I laughed aloud this time and said, as I reached into my wallet, "I really believe you when you say you could use the money. I think you must have a quota you have to reach each night. Nevertheless, I am not one of those men you run into every night. I don't need your service. I just wanted to help you get a rest. Here is the twenty I said I would give you. You take this and consider it a gift."

She would not take no for an answer. She said, "I know you're a nice guy but I want to be nice to you, too."

By now, we were coming upon the Hilton, and I asked her, "Are those your two friends there on the corner?"

She said that they were and I pulled up beside them. They were stunning. They may have been nineteen or twenty years old. They bothlooked like they had been in fitness classes all day long just to be sure, they looked their best at night.

They opened the back door and they very excitedly said, "Hi, there. We sure do thank you for the ride."

Then they started to chatter amongst themselves about what had happened in the last hour or so. There conversation lasted for about two minutes, when all of a sudden I had an idea. I pulled over into a parking lot and stopped.

They must have been surprised to see this. One of them said, "What are we stopping for?" I put the car in park and turned around sideways so I could see all of them at the same time. I smiled and hoped that I looked as excited as I felt, and said with joy, "I know what this is all about. This is a revival."

You would not believe their faces. One smiled and looked nervous. Another put her hands to the side of her head and looked as though she was in shook. The other, which I had to laugh at, put her hands up and her head back, with her face looking shocked said, (almost to herself) "Ohhhhhhh #!*&%."

I then said, after I stopped laughing, "Listen, I happen to be studying for my bachelor's degree in ministry. I didn't mean to scare you but I felt led to say that at this moment."

One of them said, "No, you listen: I ain't ever going to change anytime soon. So, you can just forget preaching to me, brother."

I laughed again, only this time I was really laughing hard. They must have thought I was making a joke, so they began to laugh as well.

I said, "I used to be out there. You know, living in the streets and doing my thing. I just happened to get it together and ask God to help me to help others. I am not going to preach to you. I just wanted to get your attention."

The girl in the back seat — the one who held up her arms and yelled

"Oh, $#^*&. "Well, you know you got my attention. $#@*&^, you made me get the attention of every son of a beach on the street. Yeah, you got my attention brother."

I laughed and so did the girls. I put the car in drive and started toward Waikiki again. The girls started joking about the whole thing and one of them asked if I would drop them off at McDonald's. I said I would and then I said, "I really love people. I want everyone I know to know what I know and to see life the way I see it. I won't preach to you ladies, but I would like to say one thing before I drop you off."

My friend next to me said, "What's that, Bob?"

"Well, you already know or think you know what is ahead in your life. However, never forget that if you want to do what is in your heart to do, all you have to do is ask the man upstairs. Don't ever forget that. If you forget everything, you have ever learned in life overnight. I hope that somehow you will be able to remember that one thing, that God loves you".

By now, we were at McDonald's and I pulled over.

I said to them as they were getting out of the car, "I love you sisters, but I could never love you as much as He does."

They all, at the same time, said thanks for everything. One of them then leaned into the car and said, "I won't forget, Bob." And off they went.

The moral of this story is that even if I travel the world and no one hears or heeds my words, this morning I felt that one person will one day remember what I said. I pray it saves her life. (A one-time incident happened. Why did it happen? I do not know, but God must have wanted one of them to get the message.)

I love you , but I could never love you as much as He does.

Brother Bob

"You're Just a Dumbbell"

Aloha, family, friends, and all of God's children,

Back in NorthDakota, when I was very young, I would often do stupid things, as any young man does. This would give my many siblings a chance to tease me and say things that hurt. One of the names they would call me was a "dumbbell." I did not even know what a dumbbell was but I knew by the why they said it that it was a bad thing. Therefore, of course, it hurt my feelings and I would retaliate.

It sure is something that we remember things like that when we become older. The reason I remember that word is something that happened to me recently and I would like to share that with you.

I flew back to Minnesota for my sister-in-law's funeral on May 25, 2004. It was a sad affair because my sister-in-law had just gone to the hospital two weeks earlier to see why her stomach was in pain. The Doctors told her she had cancer, and two weeks later, she had gone to be with the Lord.

My wife's family and all of their friends were very kind, and we all knew that Peggy had gone onto a better place. One day, I would like to tell you of this kindness of my wife Ruth's family and friends. They are truly all God's children and I love each one of them very much. They make me feel as though I had been a part of their family all of my life; I have enjoyed incredible love on their part. Ruth's twin brother, Charles, came to where Ruth and I were staying each morning and Charlie and I would go out to try our hand at fishing. I believe that it was a way for him and me to know one another better as well as mourn for Peggy. At least, that was what it was like for me. However, the word "mourn" has never pleased me. It should be more "praising Peggy" than "mourning Peggy." In addition, we, or at least I, did praise Peggy to myself as I stood on the back of the lake with my pole in hand. Peggy and I had become quite close over the years I had known her. She was a sister to me all the way. I loved her very much and I will miss her to the end.

While Charlie and I were fishing, we, of course, had our little stories of fishing and of other funny things that happened to us in our years. Now that I look back, I feel like I was a dumbbell for telling one particular story.. We all have told a story or two that we wish we had not afterward.

I told Charlie of an affair I had with an older women when I was seventeen years young. I cannot tell you the whole story because I am afraid that one day the people involved may read of this. Therefore, to protect them, I will just tell you of how I was a dumbbell.

I told Charlie of how the husband (who knew me as if he were my big brother or something like that) had come home while this older woman — his wife — and I were coupling in an obvious sin. I had to hurry and get dressed before he made it from the front door to the bedroom of, "his" house. However, I knew I would not have time to dress or make it to the back door. Therefore, I opened the window and threw my things out. Then, I jumped out, as well. I ran to the back yard and threw my things over the fence. Then I climbed up over with the sound of the husband's feet and voice behind me. He was not far behind as far as I could tell. I started to run up the road with him yelling obscenities at me from behind. (I do not think he saw my face, well, maybe one.) As I ran, I could hear from the sound of his voice that he had stopped chasing me. The last thing I heard was, "I'll get you one of these days, you ------."

When I was telling Charlie this story, I had said to him, "Now, this is funny," and I went on to tell him how the husband had chased me up the street. However, it wasn't funny at all. I could tell by the expression on Charlie's face that he did not think it was funny, either. What is funny about sleeping with another man's wife is nothing funny at all. I was a dumbbell for even thinking it would be funny to someone.

So what is the point here? It is this: even though I am a Christian, I still make mistakes. However, another thing that it showed me is that I still have not reached the point of full maturity in my walk with the Lord. We are always learning to grow and to be as much like Jesus as possible and then things like this slip in to show us our mistakes. God told me fix this mistake so I wrote to Charlie and apologized to him.

By telling you of this mistake, I am not cleaning out my guilt but I am sharing it so that you may not make a similar mistake. God has forgiven me already for my past sins but I pray that I hear and understand Him when He corrects my faults day by day. We all are very blessed indeed to have a Father who cares enough to correct us and let us mature one day at a time.

I love you, but I could never love you as much as He does.

Brother Bob

Compassion

12/17/03

Aloha family, friends and all of God's children,

The reason that I am writing this letter is to let whomever it is that is reading it see something that they may have overlooked before. That is this: We must have compassion if we wish to receive compassion. The last thing that God wants to see is you going off into a corner of your own little world and feeling sorry for yourself. We all must look up if we are to see out, beyond what our needs are and into the needs of others. Life's fulfillment is the joy of giving to those less fortunate than us. God's plan for our happiness is for us to share what we have with others. That is so wise. When we walk this path, we must have patience with others and with God our Father. If you love Him and are always faithful, you will have peace.

> Let love and faithfulness never leave you; bind them around your neck, write them on the tablet of your heart. Then you will win favor and a good name in the sight of God and man.
>
> Proverbs 3:3-4

> Trust in the Lord with all your heart and lean not on your own understanding; in all your ways acknowledge him, and he will make your path straight.
>
> Proverbs 3:5-6

We can listen and be of help to others. However, we must never forget that the one that listens to everything and everybody is our Lord. We can always feel good in our heart and soul if we have a personal relationship with the Lord. Follow where He leads, by way of the Holy Spirit.

I just finished a book written by Joyce Meyer titled How to Hear from God: Learn to Know His Voice And Make Right Decisions. A kind of book that you cannot put down once you begin to read it. Sister Joyce has a number of books on the shelf at Borders if you wish to get them.

Well, my friend, it is time to get outside and do some garden work. May your days be filled with peace and joy.

I love you, but I can never love you as much as He does.

Brother Bob and Sister Ruth

The Word

5/9/04

Aloha, my friends, family, and all of God's children,

There are those of you who, if I were to start this letter out with scripture, would put it down because you just do not want to hear (read) anything from the Bible. Nevertheless, humor me here; there is a reason for my caring. Please be patient and read through, you'll understand why.

In scripture Luke 8:15 Jesus spoke by a parable:

"A sower went out to sow his seed, some fell on the wayside; and it was trodden down, and the fowls of the air devoured it.
And some fell upon a rock; and as soon as it was sprung up, it withered away, because it lacked moisture.
And some fell among thorns; and choked it.
And other fell on good ground, and sprang up, and bore fruit a hundred-fold.
And when he had said these things, he cried; "He that hathears to hear, let him hear."

And then his disciples asked him, saying, "What might this parable be?"

If you want to know the answer to that question, you will have to look it up in your Bible. As I said, I am not writing this to preach to you but to show you something else. Here is what I want to show you. I will write the same thing that Jesus spoke to his disciples but in a way, "if Jesus was here, speaking to us right now", may say so that we understand.

This is what he may say:

"Yo, yo mama." (Just kidding.)

He would say:

"This person wanted to change his life around, so he took up the Bible. He had been forgiven of his sins and he began to understand God's ways as time went along. As he learned, he started to tell others of his new found life. However, friends told him that it was all a bunch of crap and he believed them. Therefore, he turned back to his old ways. One or two of the people he talked to at first believed what he told them and started to read the Bible and have joy. However, they did not go to church, or bother to ask anyone from church which direction they should take to learn, so they gave up and went out to party with the rest. Then also, there were those who listened to this first dude and they thought, 'This is a great scam. I could get rich off this %#$@&." Therefore, they read some of the Bible, enough to fool others into believing they were Christians, and they made money off many dudes. They did not help anyone out with all the cash they brought in. However; they sure did live the "life of Riley." There was one person who knew in his heart that what this first cat said was the truth. He knew in his heart that something new was going on inside of him. He wanted to learn more and to give more so he listened and learned from the heart. He wanted to share all that he had learned and all that was given to him with others. It was overwhelming how much love he felt in his heart and he just could not share enough.

He wanted everyone to have what he had. He knew that in order to tell it in a way that it would help others, he needed patience. He had to have patience to learn and then wait for God to tell him what to do at the right time.

Man that is heavy stuff. You can have what this cat has too if you just ask God for help. So, get it together, man, and go to church. Learn what it is all about if you want to have some peace here and some joy. Find out who and what our Father is about and you will have all that you could want just by the asking.

May you have a nice day and God bless you all".

Have you seen my point yet? It takes a man of God, someone God chooses to spread his word. It is a person who God knows wants to help others to understand His ways. There are fools who try to deceive us, but God knows who they are. There is nothing we can do about it. He has his reasons to let each of us make our own decisions, good or bad. However, we pay for our actions in the end. He has the last say about any decision we make, when we get there before him.

The beauty of this whole thing with God and Jesus is that we do have that choice. It really saddens me to think that I may not see one of my family members or one of my friends up there. In addition, if you, for one minute, think that your way is the best and only way, you are one of those that I sadly will not see. Therefore, you see, I am one of those who He chooses to tell of Him and His son. I am laughed at because I am not ashamed to tell all whom I know that He talked to me audibly. They laugh when I tell them what He said. Some do not laugh at me to my face but God allows me to see who those people are. They judge me when, in fact, He is the only judge of us all. I have days when I want to give up and Satan (there really is a Satan) tries to make a fool of me. Nevertheless, as God knows, I will not be dissuaded.

One of the things God told me is that I would need much faith and patience. I may have been thrown off my course now and then. I am not perfect, but I ask Him for help for restoration and He graces me with His love.

"What a Wonderful World."

"I love you, but I could never love you as much as He does."

Brother Bob

Brother George

Aloha family, friends and all of God's children,

Growing up with eleven brothers and sisters was fun and exciting. We did all the things other children did, but we just did them in a group or team sort of way. We didn't have to go and find other neighborhood kids to play with, we had ourselves to entertain. Climbing trees or playing tree tag, just as squirrels would do, was one of the many things I enjoyed. Then, there were the days when we would hurt one another or have accidents, just as all children do.

One day, when I was playing over in the "southforty," as we liked to call it, my brother, George called me over to see him. He said he wanted to show me something. The way George said things made you get excited about what was going to happen. He always had the best games to play and the most joyful places to go. George was five years older then I was and I loved to hang out with him whenever he would let me. I always wanted to do what my older brothers and sisters were doing, just as smaller siblings always do.

When I walked toward George, I was not paying attention to what he had in his hands. As I walked closer, I looked over at George just in time to see that he had a BB gun (rifle) pointed at me. I froze in my shoes. I knew my eyes were opened wide as I pleaded with him not to shoot me. He laughed hysterically and said he would not do that. As I watched him laughing, I heard the gun go off and then felt the pain in my chest. I must have been about fourteen feet or so from his gun sight and the BB hit me squarely in the chest. I started to cry because of the pain. I was only 6 and George was 11. Mother was the one who George would have to deal with, but as always, she did not do much. I wanted to run into the house, but George stopped me and begged for my forgiveness. Mother heard my crying and came running out. She asked what happened and George said he accidentally shot me in the chest. I said as well that it was an accident because I didn't want George to get into trouble. Little did I know then that for years later, I would be protecting of my older brother from much more than most brothers do. (I also did not know at that time, but George was a very sad, lonesome, and scared little boy).

George and I did many things together after that happened. He trusted me not to tell anyone if we did something wrong, such as breaking into the neighbor's house to steal money and cookies on our way to the James River to fish for bullheads and northern pike. I was scared but George acted as if he had done it many times, maybe he had.

When I was sixteen, George came home on leave from Vietnam. He had a month but he left after only a week and a half. I introduced him to a girl I knew and I thought they had a good thing going. Her name was Ruth, but for some reason, they parted ways. I found out after George left that he had told her he was using heroin. I did not know why he was so moody until I heard that, and it explained to me why he woke up one morning all ticked off . Mother was making him breakfast so I went to wake him up. He woke up angry. He told me to get away from him and leave him alone.

When he came downstairs, he had his sea bag packed. Mother asked him what was wrong and where was he going. George just said he was tired of being in Seattle and he wanted to go back to Vietnam. Mother started to cry and asked him to stay, but it was a waste of words. I never have told her to this day, why he was really going back. He later wrote a letter to her and told her he wanted to be with his friends in Vietnam because it was his duty. I, however, felt that there was much more to his leaving then he was telling us.

I asked George about that day one time and he said that he was having a bad withdrawal experience. When I asked him how he ever got off the stuff, he said that he went cold turkey. Then he said to me, "Bob, don't ever get hooked on that #^%2#. I tell you, coming off that stuff cold turkey is the worst thing I ever went through."

George never once talked to me about his time in, "the Nam."

However, we did talk about the days near the end of it. George used to be married to a Vietnamese woman. (Her name is Mimi, a wonderful woman who to this day still calls Mother "Mom." Mimi comes to our

Christmas party and other family gatherings. She used to be a professional singer and she would put on shows for our parents on special occasions. Mimi still is, and will always be, family.) George told me one day, after Mimi and he had been divorced for a year or so, that she needed his help. Things in Vietnam were getting hot. People there were getting out as quickly as possible because the U.S.A. was leaving Vietnam. Mimi asked George if he would go back and get her family out. She said she would pay for the flight and any expenses he had. George, of course, was the perfect person for the job because he knew Saigon inside and out. Mimi's folks and her relatives had no way out unless George went to get them. I knew he would be in big trouble there. I asked him if he was going and he said, "What would you do, Bob?"

I said, "I think I would go if I thought I could pull it off. However, knowing you, you're going to go. It doesn't matter if you think you can pull it off or not."

He laughed and said, "You know me pretty good, don't you, Robert?"

I asked him if he thought he could arrange for me to go with. He said, "Mother losing one son would be enough, if it came to that. You better stay and get a place ready for a planeload of Mimi's family."

We both laughed about that because it was his way of saying, "No problem, I'll be back in a day or two." However, inside, we both knew that it was going to be a really tough mission for him. We were trying to cover up our fear with laughter.

When he came home, we went out to get as drunk as we could. That was when he told me about the fear and sorrow that he saw. He said that as he was getting Mimi's family on the plane, there was gunfire all around them. He said that he could only get the family members on, but all the relatives were begging him to get them on as well. Mimi's father would not come. George said that he wanted to die in his own country. George said that as they were going up the stairs, he had to push and kick off Mimi's friends and relatives. When they got on the plane and took off, they almost did not get in the air because of the weight and the gunfire.

The airplane, packed to the hilt, became filled with tears. George said that they put sheets from corner to corner, or hook to hook, to make a place to lie down. (It was a cargo plane.) Some were hurt and bleeding from fighting to get to and on the plane. The people were crying, some were trying to get out to go back to be with family, and others were fighting among each other for reasons unknown to George. George said it was the saddest thing he ever saw. He started to cry when he saw a woman hit a child to shock the child into being quiet.

As we sat there in the bar, I looked at George and he had tears in his eyes. I knew George to be one of the toughest men I ever met. However, when it came to seeing someone suffer, it always broke his heart. Maybe that was one of the reasons I loved him so much: his big heart.

I believe the reason for the pain George felt for others was developed when he was young. I was about eight years old when I saw George get beat up by five members of my family. I do not want you to think that my siblings were bad; they just did not know better. What had happened was that George had said or done something wrong. I never did find out what it was that he did (or did not do), but I do remember trying to stop my older siblings from beating him. As they were hitting him, one of my older brothers hit him in the head with his fist. George went down, and as he was falling, I remember how he hit his head on the corner of a windowsill. He lay there quivering and as he lay there, the others were hitting and kicking him. One of my brothers shoved me to the floor as I tried to stop him. When George came to, they then realized that he was not pretending that he was knocked out. I was crying and I went over to George and asked him if he was ok. He did not say anything. He just looked at me with tears in his eyes. Not a sound came out of him. He looked at the others as if to say, "You may beat me, but I won't cry like a baby for you." I think it was at that time that I knew George and I were alike. I did not know how much we were alike until one day my father said to me in the heat of anger, "You're just like Pokie. (That was George's nickname). You two are bothgoing to end up in jail." Dad said those words as an insult, but I took it as a compliment: it made George and I all that much closer.

After twelve years in the army, George said he had had enough. He had come over to Seattle to visit. He was stationed in Hawaii at that time. One day, he and my older brother, Jerry, came to the machine shop I was working at. George asked me if I wanted to go back with him and Jerry to Hawaii if he paid for the flight. I was going with a girl at the time, but other than that, I saw no reason not to.

When we arrived in Hawaii, George told me Mimi was working in one of the clubs, singing. I wanted to go and see her, even if they were divorced. When we went to the club, she was on a break. George did not want to wait around, so we left. However, I could tell by his actions that he still loved her and did not want to be hurt by seeing her. That is what he did most of the time: hide his emotions. I started to see that he was doing it more and more, however.

George was married in Seattle around 1980 or so. He had two fine sons, Flint and Luke. Try as he would, he could not stop the pain and sorrow of his childhood and his time in Vietnam. He would try to cover up the pain with alcohol. Later, it would be alcohol and drugs prescribed by the veteran's hospital doctors. For twelve years, George, Jerry, and I went through things that normal brothers would never experience. We fought with one another and for one another. We went through divorces together and jail time together. We went through hospitals together and many states together. We went through sorrow together and happiness together. We laughed harder together and cried together more than any three brothers could ever have done in their lifetimes. We even hurt one another at times. However, of all these times together, there was not one time that we ever stopped loving one another. We had good reason to, but we were too close to hold anything against the other. The one thing that was different between the three of us was this: We all had heart, but George's was so much bigger, he did not ever learn how to use it. With the sorrow he felt, he just could not make his heart work with it. He was paralyzed with sadness and he knew it. He turned his life around when he gave his heart to God. He quit drinking and stopped smoking cigarettes. He tried to tell me about God's ways and how He could make a difference in my life if I wanted Him to. However, I was a fool and I thought I knew it all. I was one of those people who thought God was for the weak. I should have listened to George; I would have saved myself a lot of heartache.

Nevertheless, after a year of being sober and a family man, something happened to change his direction. When he started to drink again, it was downhill. Here was a man who wanted nothing more than to help others, but he could not help himself. What makes a man like that? Could it be fear, doubt, sorrow, pain, anger, sadness, guilt, or maybe a broken heart? I think George felt all of the above. He was paralyzed between hope and sorrow. However, it was George's choice to lose faith not God giving up on him.

Today, we have a war in a country not too much unlike Vietnam, maybe not the same fighting situation, but similar in other respects. Again, there will be troops coming home who have been wounded or paralyzed. They may be with out all of their body parts or caught between hope and sorrow, paralyzed. How are we going to treat them? What will we be able to do for them? I know of two things to help them. One of them, if possible, is to lead them to the Lord. The other is to give them what the Vietnam veterans did not get: respect. Solders are criticized for what is going on in the prison camps in Iraq. However, please, do not try to judge all for a few other's mistakes. In fact, do not judge at all. More important, don't give up on them.

George called me here in Hawaii when he lived in Seattle. He was drunk when he called and he asked me if he could come and live with me. I had been sober for three months and I felt that should he come over here, I would drink again. So I said, "I can't do that, George, I'll start drinking again."

He said, "We can get a place on the beach and take life easy for a while."

I told him I could not. (It was one of the few times I said no to him.)

He said, "You're just like all the rest of the Dunham's," and he hung up the phone. Two weeks later, I received a call from one of my brothers telling me that George was gone. That is when I started to drink again for the next four years. I became homeless again, living my life as George did, to his end. Now, I was the one paralyzed between hope and sorrow.

By the grace of God, I am here to tell this story of a truly great man. No one knew him as I did, except God. One thing I learned, from the day that I gave my life to God, is this: "No man is an island." George went home to the Lord. I am here to see to it that it was not in vain. I will not say no to anyone who comes to me for help. No matter what it takes, George's life will live on through me. I will do for God what He had intended for George. I am blessed to have had George for a brother, but more so, to have had him as a friend. I am no longer paralyzed. In addition, if I can help any of the soldiers who come home from Iraq, in any way, I will do it with much joy and happiness. Will you do that, also? God wants us to help one another, why not help these men and women just a little more. Let us not leave any paralyzed left behind.

"I love you, but I could never love you as much as He does."

Brother Bob

By the way: George's sons are doing great. They are getting to know their father through family members and me. I like to think that George left behind two angels. I love them as if they where my own. I am grateful to the Lord for having them in my life.

Whose Dreams Are They Anyway?

Aloha family, friends and all of God's children,

I woke up this morning and tried to figure out what my dream was about. You know how it goes: You start to stir just before you wake up and you are half-asleep and half-awake. You struggle to see who that is in your dream and why you are in that certain situation. It may be a nightmare or it could be a love story. There are many things we dream about.

Quite often, I wake up singing a song. For example, this morning I awoke singing, "Do You Believe in Magic," by the group The Loving Spoonful. I had been dreaming of two of my nephews, Flint and Luke. Why I was dreaming of Flint and Luke, I had no idea. However, I do know this: I will call them today just to say hello. Maybe that is what dreams are for, to remind us of someone. On the other hand, maybe they are to remember to do something. Then again, maybe they are to bring us joy when needed. I did not feel the need for God to put a song in my heart this morning because today is Saturday. On Saturday mornings, the first thing I do (after praying) is to turn on the fishing channel. God brings joy to my heart and the fishing channel brings joy to my eyes.

Therefore, this morning, I am sitting back with my cup of coffee, with joy in my heart, and seeing a nice, big striped bass being caught down in Mexico. As I am rocking in my chair, I am singing, "Do you believe in magic, of a young girl's heart," and then I go on mumbling the rest of the words because I can't remember them.

I am trying to focus on the anglers, but I just cannot help but try to figure out why I am singing that particular song. Then I get the answer: I feel that God was telling me that in those days of my youth, I did at times think those days were magical. After all, I was just a boy, a dreamer of hope with excitement, a lad with the desire to be somebody or do something to help others. But alas, they all soon disappeared as each year passed. When the anger and the pain came, I found myself listening to music to drown out the sorrow. The magic was gone.

Flint and Luke are the sons of my brother, George. As you know, George and I had a close relationship. When George left us to be with the Lord, I told myself that I would do whatever I could to help the boys. I had found out through the family grapevine that the government said that George's wife and children could not get government benefits after George went to be with the Lord. Now, I knew the story why George wanted out of the army, and I was with him when he went to his superior officer to ask for an early release.

In 1972, I was in Honolulu, where George had been stationed at the time. My older brother Jerry, George, and I had just flown back to Hawaii from Seattle after George had been there on leave. After being in Hawaii for about a month or so, George told us he was going to get out of the service. I told him he could not do that unless he accepted a, lessthan-desirable discharge instead of an honorable discharge. Of course, George was well aware of this and told me so. However, he also said that he could not take it anymore. At the time, this was happening, the term, "Post Traumatic Stress Disorder," or PTSD, had not materialized in the military vocabulary.

I had no idea what kinds of benefits were available at that time upon discharge, but I had a feeling that George may be losing some of them if he accepted this type of discharge. However, I still felt that his family should receive all that those with honorable discharges received, as far as it went for college for the boys and some kind of benefits to his wife, Hilda. So, when I found out from my siblings that George's family was to receive nothing, I became quite angry. To me, it felt like disrespect toward my brother. It was time for some magic again. Maybe I still believed in magic, even as an adult, now that I look back at this story.

Anyway, I started to write letters. I wrote to my congressional representatives, my senator, the chief of staff at the White House, the vice president, and the president of the United States. The more negative reaction I received, the more letters I wrote. Then one day, one of my brothers told me, "Bob, you have to stop writing all those letters. Hilda said that she was told that if you didn't stop writing them, the government wouldn't give her anything."

This really ticked me off. Therefore, I wrote one last letter to the general in charge of all military personnel. I cannot remember his name, or for that matter, any of the names of those I wrote to, but I do recall that he was a very honest and fair man. I thought if anyone could or would do anything about this matter, it would be him.

I told the general of George's love for his country and his fellow man. I spoke of George's sorrow whenever he came home on leave, before I joined the Marine Corps so I could go over to Vietnam to fight by his side. What I did, to make a long story short, is to tell the general that this family deserved the gifts of war. George paid the price with his PTSD and his life because of this illness.

The letter was from the heart. There was no magic in it. However, as I look back I do know that God was in it. Nothing was said for some time, or at least I did not hear anything. This was because I was, "out there" now. By saying, "out there," I mean I was now the one with PTSD, but I did not know this at the time. (It was twenty-two years later, when the doctors would give me the same diagnosis they gave George.)

I did happen to hear through the family grapevine that the kids, Flint, Luke, and as well Hilda, his wife, had financial help and one of the boys was going to college. I was so happy that day. Was it a dream come true? Was it magic? Was it a roll of the dice or just plain luck? What do you think? On the other hand, do you think it was possible that they grew tired of me writing letters.

Whose dreams are these that we dream each night? I will tell you whose they are, in my opinion: God's. What gave me the desire to write this story in the first place? Everything belongs to God. Our hearts, our minds, our bodies, and everything we see and hear. How could George's family have received these things if not by the Grace of God? There is no other answer. If God had not laid that dream into my brain, I never would have told or even thought about telling you this story. I share things with you that God put into my heart. I believe that He wants you to hear something that He is trying to tell you. Not all of you, of course, but someone who is reading this story right this moment is getting an answer to their question. Now, who can manage to do something like that other than God? It was his plan, and his timing, that you received the answer, so who other than He should receive glory for it!

Next time you have a dream, think about it for a moment, and say to yourself, "I wonder why that dream was put there."

"I love you, but I could never love you as much as He does."

Brother Bob

"And in This Corner"

Aloha, family, friends and all of God's children,

Whenever someone has left an impression on you, somehow, you just cannot seem to forget that person. It was with Mike, in the seventh grade, for me. He was a nice kid, I thought. I had been transferred from the sixth grade to the seventh grade because of some tests they gave me, in the middle of the semester when I met Mike. (They told me I was too smart for the sixth grade so I had to go to a new school. My first grade teacher had flunked me, as well as my sixth grade teacher in New Bedford, a.k.a. "Mayberry," NorthDakota. The teachers in that town just did not like me. I believe my older brothers had something to do with that as well as myself. Nevertheless, those teachers caused a lot of strife in my life.)

I had only been in this new classroom for about three days when I first saw Mike. He walked into the classroom, and he was about ten minutes late.

The teacher, Mr. K, said to Mike, "You're supposed to come into my classroom on time, Lindale."

Mike did not look at Mr. K; he just kept on walking in and said in a low voice, "It's all a bunch of bull#%^#&*, anyway."

Mr. K became red in the face and he acted as if he was going to start to hyperventilate. He very quickly walked over to Mike, grabbed his arm and said, "Let's go outside."

About five minutes later, Mike came trough the door first and you could see the red in his eyes from the tears. His face was red and I wondered if Mr. K had hit him. When Mike walked in, the class began to laugh at him. That really made me mad, so I said, "Why don't all of you shut up and leave him alone."

Mr. K was right behind Mike and if I had thought he was hyperventilating before then; this must have been close to a heart attack. No one talked like that in his classroom but him. He yelled at me to come outside.

I went down the three steps, with Mr. K walking in front of me. I could have sworn he was so shaky he was going to fall down the steps. After all, "no one" talked like this in "his" classroom. However, I didn't know that. I had only been in his classroom for three days. I should have known better however. In NorthDakota, you did not say a word. Maybe, I was changing because it was a new town and new school.

As we walked over to where no one could see us from any other classroom, he turned around and slapped me. It was a good slap but I had had worse from my Dad. I did not pay much attention to it, so this angered him even more. Therefore, he balled up his fists and hit me as hard as he could in the stomach. That hurt. I bent over, gasping for air. I think he must have started to worry because when I looked up to give him a dirty look, he looked at me as if he was worried. I then had a few tears in my eyes from the pain, and he said, "You don't say anything to anybody about this or I'll get you kicked out of school."

When I walked into the classroom, no one would look at me, and I said, "Are you happy now?" I do not know if Mr. K had heard me say it or not, but if he did, he did not say anything to me.

The class was quiet the rest of the time we were there. When we walked out afterwards, Mike walked over to me and said, "Hey, what's your name?"

Before I could answer he said, "Man, no one has ever stuck up for me like that before. That was really something. Do you want to come over to my place after school and do something?"

I laughed and said that he should not have been picked on. Even though I knew he was in the wrong, I felt the class should not have laughed at him and I told him so.

After school, as we were walking to his house, I listened to what he had to say. He seemed to be very angry at the whole world. I was wondering why as we walked into his front yard. Mike said, "Just a minute while I go tell my folks I'm home."

As he walked in, he acted as if it was an emergency that he tells his folks he was home. I heard some shouting in the house and thought maybe the school had called his folks to tell them what went on today in our classroom. When Mike came out, he looked like he had been crying again. He tried to keep his head down and as we started to walk away from the front steps, he said, "I'm going to get away from that drunken s.o.b. and I won't have to put up with this s--- any more. I'll see you later, Bob, I have to go somewhere. I'll talk to you later." Then, he went out over a field we had reached and never looked back.

I did not see Mike in school the next day. Mr. K asked me if I saw him and I told him in a smart-alecky tone of voice, "He's probably late again, Mr. K."

Mr. K gave me a dirty look and stopped the questions. I never saw Mike again. I do not know if he ran away or if his parents took him to another school. Then about two days later, Mr. K said that Mike would no longer be in our class. He didn't say why or what happened to him, just, "Mike won't be in our classroom any more."

I have often wondered what happened to Mike, but as I look back, I could see in Mike just what I would become just two years later. I became the rebel that Mike was. I soon began to have no respect for my peers or for myself. I became the alcoholic that my dad was and I had his temper. I would fight with anyone, just like Dad would do. I became my father. I wonder if Mike did as well.

We cannot go through life as children if we do not have a mentor or a father figure or someone to show us the guidelines. Are you (the person who is reading this right now) a young person? Do you have troubled child? Do you know some child who has no one to go to for comfort? Well, may I make a suggestion, if you are any of the above? Please, reach out to someone. If you are young and angry with no one to help you along, find someone. If you are an adult, help that child no matter what he or she has done to wrong you. That child needs your help. In addition, in the process of helping them, please take him or her to church. They may not grasp the meaning or be able to focus on the Lord right now, but they will remember what you did down the line. More importantly, they will know God was with them back when, "in the day."

"And that from a child thou has know the Holy Scriptures, which are able to make thee wise unto salvation through faith which is in Christ Jesus."

II Timothy 3:15

"I love you, but I could never love you as much as He does."

Brother Bob

Abraham and Us

Aloha, family, friends and all of God's children,

One of the many things that man has acquired, by man's hand, is the television. Even though it is by man's hand, it is good for God's purpose, such as to spread His word throughout the lands near and far; such was the case this day. As I sat to rest my hands of much laborious work, I happened to see the movie in which was Abraham, father of the nations and many sons who were to be Kings. God speaks of Abraham and what he wished for Abraham to do in the Word. As it is written, Abraham became the father of many. As I looked upon this man of God, I saw that God had spoken to him audibly, such as he did to me, another humble servant to our Father God. I care not who shall believe me when I speak only the truth of that day. For I know my God, our Father, with in my heart.

When Abraham's wife gave birth to Isaac, and I saw all that our Father had told Abraham had come true, my strength was once again restored.

Even though we read the Bible repeatedly, we still gain strength from it with each word. Each time we read, we read something we had missed from the readings before.

Be as Abraham was in days of old and have the faith, as he had when God told him to sacrifice his son. Trust in Him with all your heart and soul. With our Father's love, and His son Jesus as our example, and for all those who gave their lives for us as Jesus did, how could we give up on the desires of His heart, to love Him as much? We cannot.

"I love you, but I could never love you as much as He does."

Brother Bob

Living in the Path of a Storm

Aloha, family, friends, and all of God's children,

When I was homeless for so many years, it seemed to me that I was always aware of a storm brewing. By that, I mean that I felt I had to watch my back at all times because of the fear of the unexpected. Nevertheless, as I told you in past letters, "I am not going back to where I used to be. I am going forward to where I have never been before." One of the things I must do in order to stay one-step ahead is to not be hardened. "I must not have a hardened heart." I recall that when I was around twenty-four years young, I worked at a machine shop in Seattle. My job was to go around and pick up all the shavings from the machines that had been running. This job consisted of going from machine to machine and meeting each man running it. One of those men was my older brother, Jerry.

One day when I was up on the second floor of the building, I could hear all of this confusion going on down below me. I asked someone what had happened and I was told that a steel plate had landed on someone's foot. I paid no attention to it and went on with my work. Then a machinist I had become friends with came to me and asked if I had a brother who worked in the shop. I told him I did and he said he thinks it was Jerry who was injured. I ran down to the floor below and they told me that Jerry was out in a truck out back. I went out and saw Jerry sitting in the passenger seat of the truck. I then asked what had happened. His leg was shaking and his foot covered with blood. He gave me the details and the driver took off for the hospital.

After they drove off, I heard my friend call me to go out for lunch. We finished lunch and started to go back to the shop and wrap up the day. As we drove, my friend lit up a joint (marijuana), and he asked if I wanted a drag. I told him I did not trust myself with the steel if I smoked any of it. When we arrived back at work, the day went smoothly, for about an hour.

Then, the foreman came to see me. He told me he wanted to talk to me outside. We walked out and he said to me, "I know you have been smoking drugs at lunch time so I'm going to have to fire you." I could not believe I was hearing this. I must have looked like I was ready to kill him because he backed up a few steps and called into the shop for help.

I admit that I had a temper. However, my temper would only rise when I knew that there was a major injustice occurring. I must have been hyperventilating because I could see this foreman was shaking in his boots. This man had real fear in his heart.

He had good reason to have fear: I was ready to hurt him very, very badly. However, to my good fortune, three men came out and surrounded him for protection. I say "to my good fortune" because I would have gone to prison for sure for attempted murder if I had fought him.

I think that that is one (if not the one) incident that broke the camel's back for me. That may have been the start of a hardened heart. I say this because I started to have more hate for life and people than I already had. Today, I cannot even believe there is room in the heart for the word "hate." How can I hate with Jesus in my life? It is very impossible.

In Hebrews 3:8, it says, "Harden not your hearts, as in the provocation, in the day of temptation in the wilderness."

In Hebrews 3:13, it says, "But exhort one another daily, while it is called today; lest any of you be hardened through the deceitfulness of sin."

Anger, revenge, and hate are evil indeed. Nevertheless, these things, I had in my heart all the time. Therefore, I would drink and go on doing more and more sinful things. I was just surviving, one day at a time, my way (and Satan's, too). As I lived and walked in the path of the storm, I was very aware of my mistakes and my anger. I didn't care. I had no reason to care, nor did I want peace according to society's rules. My heart was so hard that I could not see beyond the pain. These feelings did not come overnight; they did not start up one day, unexpectedly. It was because of years of sorrow since I was a lad of six. I was too young to know what lay in wait. With so many brothers and sisters in my family, and an alcoholic father, there was no one in my life to guide me in the matters of the heart. It was not until I asked our true Father for forgiveness and received Jesus Christ into my heart that I understood just what the heart was supposed to feel.

You may say, "Oh, sure; just ask God for help and everything is hunky dory." I am not saying that, however, I am saying that with Jesus, you will know the truth and the truth will set you free from a hardened heart. It is as simple as that. Some of you who are reading this letter I have known for nearly all of my life. I know some of you better than you know yourselves. Nevertheless, I cannot try to convince you of why it is to your benefit, and to the benefit of each of those, you love so dearly, that God's way is the only way to live. However, by sharing with you my most personal life experiences, I am hoping that the love we have for one another is proof enough of my honesty and loyalty to you, and that you will at least think about what has happened to me in my life. I do not live on a stormy path any longer. I only wish to succeed by walking His path instead.

Benjamin Disraeli once said, "The secret to success is constancy of purpose." My purpose, just as everyone who walks the Lord's path, is to love others. We can do this by sharing what has happened in our lives with others. We can get out of the storm and walk in the light, the truth, and the joy of our new life. I am truly born again into a new life. What more joy could I have? (There is none.)

Many times, I have to laugh to myself when I am studying the Bible because I know so little. For instance, I just found out the reason Moses had a speech impediment. I am so naïve that I believed that he just did not want to talk to the pharaoh. However, in truth, when he was an infant in the Egyptian pharaoh's court, he put a hot coal in his mouth and burned his tongue. (This is not widely publicized, but it is true, according to Biblical authorities.)

The little things like this keep me reading page after page of the great book.

When you rise in the morning and cross the path of an unknown person, greet them with a smile and wish them a happy day. That is what life is all about. Do not do as it says in Proverbs 28:14 which says:

"He that blesseth his friend with a loud voice, rising early in the morning, it shall be counted a curse to him."

Stay off the path with the storms and walk with peace. If you take one day at a time and be happy for what you have, people will want to walk the path you are on and not the path of storms and pain.

"I love you, but I could never love you as much as He does."

Brother Bob

We All Know the Difference Between Right and Wrong

Aloha family, friends, and all of God's children,

I dreamt last night two men propositioned me while out in the middle of nowhere. That was a strange dream. When I woke up, I thought about my youth and how many times I had been either abused by homosexuals or how they had tried to take advantage of me because of my age.

The first time was at the zoo. To make a long story short, I made the mistake of giving this man my parents' phone number and when he called, my mother was smart enough to know what this person's intentions were, and put a stop to it. The second time, I was in a record store in the university district of Seattle, Washington. My friends, my brother, and later, I found out that we had brothers who knew this record store where we could steal tickets to big-name concerts. One time the Beatles were going to come to town and one of my friends, his older brother, and two other friends of mine went to steal these tickets. The older brother said that one of us younger kids would have to go into the bathroom and keep this person busy so the older brother could steal the tickets.

There were four of us. I had only been hanging out with these other kids for about a year and a half by this time. I had come to Seattle from NorthDakota, so I still was not too smart on how the big city worked. I was about fifteen then and I was still gullible. My friends and this older brother talked me into distracting this man in the bathroom.

I asked them what and how I was supposed to do this. They more or less convinced me he was a pushover and that he was gay. I said, "What to you mean, he's gay?" They laughed and said he likes little kids. I said, "No way. This guy is too big for me to fight if he tries to touch me." I still had not known even what "gay" meant but I knew it was something bad or one of these friends would be going in.

One of my friends said, "Hey Dunham, don't worry about it. We will be right outside the door and you just yell if he tries anything." I asked them how long I was supposed to keep him in there, and the older brother said, "All you have to do is listen for my voice. When I start to sing, 'Ding Dong the Witch is Dead,' you will know that I have the tickets and you get out of there."

I agreed, but I did not like the setup. I mean this person was about six-foot-four and weighed about 240 pounds. He was not fat at all, but in good shape. I was street smart enough to know how to fight, steal, and lie, but I had not been in a spot like this before. When you are young and you want to impress your peers, you will do just about anything to look cool. So I agreed, thinking that they would protect me. That was stupid thinking, because this person could kick all of our little butts at the same time.

Therefore, we walked into the store and the older brother introduced each of us to this man. The man asked us if we would like a drink and, of course, we all said sure. He took us to the back room of the store and poured us a drink. He went back to the front of the store because he heard the bell ring when someone entered. When he left, we gulped down a few drinks very quick. The man came back and the older brother told him that I wanted to talk to him alone in the bathroom. The man said that he would be happy to talk to me. He led me to the door and opened it. I was very nervous. When he opened the door, he seemed to push me in. As soon as the door closed, he grabbed my zipper to my jeans and started to pull it down. I slapped his hand and asked him what he was doing. He grabbed me by the neck and told me to shut up, or I would regret it. He then started to molest me.

In about one minute or so, I heard the older brother start to sing the song, "It must be the season of the witch, it must be the season of the witch." Moreover, I thought to myself that someone must have come in the store because he could not have had time to steal the tickets already. However, I didn't care if he had them or not. I wanted out of there. I yelled, "Hey, are you guys ready to go?" The man looked up at me and gave me a look that he was going to hurt me.

Just then one of my friends said, "Hey, Dunham, what are you doing in there?"

I said, "We'll be right out. I will be right there. No problem."

The man opened the door slowly, but at least it was opening. He must have been scared of someone seeing him in the act and reported to the police. As he turned to open the door, I zipped up my fly. When we came out, one of my friends asked what we were doing in there. I had a feeling that they knew exactly what this person was doing, so I did not say anything. I started to walk out and the older brother asked me where I was going. I said I had to get home or I would be in trouble.

We left the store and the older brother said, "What happened? I haven't got the tickets yet."

I said, "I'm not going back in there again. I did what you wanted. You're just too slow."

The brother then said, "I told you that when I start to sing 'The Season of the Witch,' that is when we would get the tickets."

I said, "I thought you said you were going to sing after you got the tickets."

He was mad that I did not understand him but he thought that I had just not heard him right. I heard him right. I just knew that if I did not get out of there that this person would have done more to me than he already had.

As my friends and I parted ways with the older brother, they asked me what happened in the bathroom. I told them that if I ever see that man again, when I get older, I was going to put him in the hospital. They pushed for more information, but I was too embarrassed to tell them all that happened and I was afraid to fight this person because he was too big. I was also aware that they would not be able to help me anyway. That was my first encounter with a gay man. I had a real hatred for them after that.

I was introduced by the same friend's to another older man who was gay. The only difference about this time and the last is that I was one year older and prepared to use my better judgment. This man would buy us a case of beer and let us drink it at his home. He thought he was pretty clever. However, by now, I had figured out how these people worked kids and I turned the tables on him and worked him. I would pretend that I thought he was a cool person and con him out of anything I wanted just by teasing him as the girls would do us. I would make him promises of a "date" and then I would come up with an excuse why I could not make it. Just like the girls would do to us boys to get what they wanted. He was easy.

The next encounter was in the Marine Corps. I went into town on leave to see a movie. This was in the bad part of town but I did not know this at the time. I had been sitting in my seat for about five minutes and this man came in and sat beside me. Right away, I thought that this person might be trouble, because as I looked down the aisle, I could see that he could have had a choice of about ten other seats. He was going to be trouble; I just knew it.

The movie started and it looked like it was going to be a good John Wayne flick. After about ten minutes into the movie, this person's knee hits my knee. I thought to myself that it just might be an accident, so I let it go. Then he did it again about another minute later. I again let it go as a mistake. Then he did it a third time. I thought to myself, now what would John Wayne do in a situation like this? I started to laugh at my own humor and then he did it again. As I turned around to him, I grabbed him by the throat. This was my chance to get back at all the times these kinds of men had tried to take advantage of my youth. I was no longer a little kid who weighed about a hundred and thirty pounds. I was not the skinny kid who got beat up by the bullies any longer. I wanted my revenge and this person was in my face.

As I tightened my grip around his jugular, I said to him, "If you don't get up and walk out of here with in the next two seconds, I'm going to kill you." He looked at me with fear of death in his eyes. He started to shake and tried to stand up as I tightened my grip around his throat. I loosened my grip so he could speak.

He said, "I'm…I'm…sor…sor…sorry." I then let go of him. As he started to walk out of the aisle the other direction from me, I could see he was leaving along with him a wet trail. I started to laugh as I looked up at John Wayne on the screen and I tipped my hat to him as if he could see me. I laughed about that the rest of the movie.

There were other times I had encounters with these kinds of men over the years. I even chased one around a car in broad daylight when he was in his birthday suit. Now, that one story was a very funny story.

All of these stories were funny, at the time. Today, it saddens me to no end. These men are grown men. How did they get that way? How is it that, these men as adults, still do not know the difference between right and wrong? "They do know the difference, Brother Bob...," you may say to me.

Ok, I know this and you know this, but why do they still do it? I will tell you. Just as an alcoholic has a need for the booze, these people have a need for attention. Not only that, but they have very troubled minds. Does that not sadden you? Listen, I have friends today who are gay. I have helped people who are gay. I never at any time, when I was younger, thought that I would one day be helping people who hurt me when I was young. How do people who are gay; pedophiles, murderers, or drug addicts get to that point in their lives? They were not born that way. Therefore, something must have happened to make them do something that they know is wrong and not care about what the result may bring to them.

Just think about these poor people when they die. What are they going to say to God? Are they going to say, "Sorry, Lord; I didn't know what I was doing?" We do not even believe that because we know it is not true. So what happens to them? God cannot say to him or her, "Well, that's okay; you can go over there with all the other sinners who did what you did and spend the rest of your eternalized life partying with them."

These people all have a choice in life. He gave us choice. Why would anyone want to live their life doing what they know is wrong? I have never known the answer to that question for forty-five years. I thought I knew everything about life. I was right and you were wrong. I knew the difference between right and wrong. Nevertheless, I found out that knowing the difference between the two is not enough. In order to make the changes that we need to make to get out of anything we know to be wrong, we need to have help from someone who knows more than us; someone who is stronger and more real than real itself. (You know who that is, as well.) I am not telling you anything you do not already know. You would not even be reading this book right now if you were not searching for an answer to something or other.

You know, I was watching this TV channel the other day and it showed these men who were at one time gay. I thought to myself,

"How is it that I'm watching this at this time and this day?" That is what happens when God is trying to tell us something. He will bring something across your path that you need to know about or He wants you to know about it for one reason or another. That show had some remarkable stories of how these men wanted to change but were afraid to or did not know who to ask for help. When they asked God, their problems had been solved by Him.

It always amazes me when I hear stories like theirs because each time I hear one; it is more powerful than the one before. God really loves to help us. Why would He not, we are His children.? Then I had this dream. When I woke up, He told me to tell you about how much hate I once had for these people and how He changed me into a person who cares instead of one who hates. It is amazing.

Sometimes I wonder why He chose me to tell you of the things I have learned. However, it all makes sense, because they are things that are for real and from the heart. He knows my heart, so He is going to let me help those who want to listen and want to change. If a person did not want to have a better life, they would not read this. Or it may go in one ear and out the other. If you think you know everything, like I used to think, this book will not be helpful. I pray you are not that kind of person.

I pray you believe me, because I have nothing to gain by telling you my life story. I have only one thing in mind when it comes to you: I hope that you ask Him for help. I may make mistakes in life as time goes on. I know I will, in fact. However, hey, the mistakes will not be on purpose because just like you, I know the difference between right and wrong.

As always, I will end this letter from my heart with,

"I love you, but I could never love you as much as He does."

Brother Bob

My Guardian Angel Was Rejoicing

Aloha family, friends and all of God's children,

Rain clouds filled the sky as I walked down the street. "I hope it doesn't start raining until I reach the theater," I thought to myself. I had no idea what was playing out but I felt that on such a cloudy night it would be nice to take my girlfriend out. Just as I reached the theater, the rain started to come down. I called Ruth to ask her if she would like to join me, but before I could tell her what was playing, she said to me, "Bob, I don't know what it is but I have this overwhelming feeling that your supposed to come over to my place right now."

"Why would you tell me such a thing?" I said with a smile on my face. I remembered that she had told me things before that were spiritual. Therefore, I was very interested to know more.

She said, "I just can't understand why, but you must come now."

I agreed, even though I was not looking forward to walking in the rain. Ruth lived only nine blocks away. If the rain should get any heavier, I would be asking her to use her robe and dryer the minute I walked into her home.

I had only walked about forty yards from the theater when a car pulled up along the side of the road and stopped beside me. "Someone looking for directions," I thought to myself. Then all of a sudden, the passenger side of the car opened up. I heard a woman's voice say, "Get in and I'll give you a ride to wherever you're going." This comment surprised me and I leaned over to look inside, with caution. To my surprise, I saw a woman that had a glow about her and a smile to match.

Now, to some, this may seem to be a little too hard to believe, but she knew all about me. Maybe not all, but she knew some of what happened to me, so therefore, I began to think that she may know more. She said to me, "Take my hand; I want to tell you something." She caught me off guard. I looked at her and she still had that smile. I did not know what to think. Then, I thought about my conversation with Ruth about rushing right over to see her.

I slid into the car, looked at her and said, "I'd like to thank you for the ride but I'm only going about nine or ten blocks. Did I hear you right? You said you have something to tell me?"

She grinned at me and said, "Yes, I do. I am so happy for you." Then she reached over and put her hand on mine where I had it on the car seat. She said, "I have wonderful things to tell you. You are so blessed. The Lord has such wonderful plans ahead. He wanted me to tell you that you will indeed be traveling around the globe. You will help so many people in your life here. I know that God has things planned that you were not sure of."

She then went on to tell me all that the Lord had told me audibly back in 1995. I could hardly believe my ears. If ever there was confirmation to a prayer, this certainly was it. God had spoken to me in February of 1995 and it was now about four months later. I had lost my job and had to move out of my apartment. I could not afford rent so I was living out of the back of my van. I was starting to lose hope, to be honest with you. Nevertheless, I was losing it faster than I realized it or God would not have sent this angel.

As I write this letter, it just now occurred to me that my brother George died about a week or two after this angel came to me. When George died, I started to drink again, and I drank for four more years and was homeless all four of those years. Then, of course, just as God and the angel had said, I was delivered from the alcohol when I stepped out of Tripler Medical Building for Veterans. God had sent this angel to tell me that no matter what happens in the years to come, that I had in fact heard His voice and He confirmed it through this angel. That is amazing. God is so smart, and has so much Grace. He knew that I would drink so He prepared me. In fact, when I was "out there" I was taking homeless people with me to the back of my church (at that time it was Word of life) and telling them they needed to hear what He had to say. There is a cemetery behind the church. One time, as we were sitting there, one of the other homeless men said to me, "Brother, what are we doing sitting here in the cemetery, listening to this preacher, anyway?"

I told him, "You remember how I told you God talked to me? Well, I believe that if you listen to this man talking about God that you will get at least one thing out of what this preacher is saying that will help you. You know I don't lie, so you know that God really talked to me. So if I tell you that He wants you to hear something, I think you would be wise to listen. Besides, I'm the one furnishing the bottle of booze here, aren't I?" Then I smiled and told them that they really will get something out of this if they just take an hour to do so. We did that for about three months. Some of the men dropped out or they would not come unless I had some booze, but I know that sitting in that cemetery did change some of them in some way. Glory is to God.

Now, back to the angel. As we neared the stoplight, after we had only gone three and a half blocks, I told her I would get out at the light. She said that she had much more to tell me if I wished to hear it. However, I felt so overwhelmed by it all that I really did not know what to say. Therefore, I just said no thank you as we came to the light that was already red. I stepped out of the car and it all of a sudden hit me, "That was an angel, Bob. That's why Ruth said she didn't know why I had to come right away; there was such a short time involved."

As I turned to tell her, that I wanted to hear more, the light had already changed and she was gone. I thought to myself, "How can that be? I had been standing there less then a half a minute. Where was she?" I did not see the car she was in and I thought to myself that maybe she wasn't even there to begin with. "Am I going crazy or something?" Nevertheless, I knew it did happen. In addition, I felt this enormous kind of joy and love for God. I knew God had sent this angel. I know, that I know, that I know, that I had just been given Grace once again.

I am in no way bragging about God speaking to me or sending me an angel. I just want to share this with others so they too can know that God speaks to anyone who wants to hear Him. I have learned so much since those times. I have come to know how to hear God daily but not always am I right. I mean, sometimes, I may think its God but of course, it is the Holy Spirit working through me and with our Lord. However, each day that I live, I wait with such excitement of what is to come and what it is that I may hear from our Father. We children of God are blessed to have such a wonderful Father to watch over us. I, for one, can in no way put into words the love that I have for Him.

I pray that each person who reads this story thank Him for all that He does every day.

"I will make them and the places all around my hill a blessing; and I will cause showers to come down in their season; there shall be showers of blessings.

Ezekiel 34:26

I pray that with all that happens to me in the future, I will be ever so humble and grateful for His guidance and wisdom. You and I may not be perfect, but we have someone watching over us who is and He wants only what is best for us.

I love you, but I could never love you as much as He loves us.

Brother Bob
(A grateful child of God)

Hit Me with Your Best Shot

Aloha, family, my friends and all of God's children,

At one time, I was known as the best rock thrower in the town of New Rockford, NorthDakota. I was riding on cloud nine, watching other kids envy me, whenever I hit a crow off a telephone line. When all the kids in the neighborhood would chose teams for a rock fight, I was the number one pick. How exciting it was to be able to throw a rock from fifty or ninety yards and hit another kid in the head.

"Then it happened, the discovery of the slingshot". (The greatest invention since the rubber band gun.) I was Robin Hood with a weapon better than the bow and arrow. I was David looking out around corners for my Goliath. I thought to myself that if Davy Crocket and I had a contest, he with his rifle, Betsy, and me with one of my best-chosen rocks, I would win easily. I would at least hit him with my best shot.

We all had our dreams when we were young. You wanted to be the best. You wanted to be recognized for something. However, I was also angry when I was young. Most of that anger came from lack of attention. With eleven brothers and sisters, it was hard to get attention and feel loved. I imagine that most children get plenty of attention, unless their father is an alcoholic. Then all the attention becomes focused on what was going to happen to you next. If you have no guidance from an adult, you grow up figuring out what you are supposed to do on your own. That can, as it did in my case, cause much distress and anger.

When I was talking to the Lord this morning about those memories, a thought suddenly came to me: "Is it coming across to people that I pity myself when I write of these things?" I sure did not want or intend to do such a thing. I do not want people feeling sorry for me. After all, that is what I tried to avoid all of my life. Therefore, I had a feeling that the Lord wanted me to make it clear that I have no self-pity. These letters are not intended to divert attention to me in any way. These letters are to, hopefully, give praise to God for what he had taught me and what he is teaching me each day. A Christian is honored to tell of, "His Grace", in all that has happened to him.

So now, with that out of my system, let me continue with my story.

I was like "Dennis the Menace" in those days. The only difference between Dennis and me is that I had older brothers to protect me if I got into trouble, such as the time one day when I had to fight an older kid. I used to deliver the town paper for an older kid who gave me a quarter each time I sold one. I would go down the streets of town in New Rockford with excitement running wild to make those quarters. I would walk into the bars and occasionally, I would get an extra dime or a few extra pennies. Occasionally, my dad would be in the bar playing cards with his friends. The men would tease Dad, but I could tell it was all in fun, because I knew my dad had a reputation as a very good fighter.

However, one day, Dad did not feel like laughing and told a man to keep quiet, in a drunken slurring way, with much cussing. The other man got up and told Dad to step outside to fight. Dad just stood up and said, "Hit me with your best shot."

The man swung and my dad ducked. Just as the other man's arm went past Dad's head, Dad hit him in the mouth.

The man was stunned at first and then he said, "Sorry Mort, I shouldn't have said anything." Dad looked at me and told me to get out and sell my papers.

I learned something that day: let the other person swing, duck, and then run. (Just kidding.)

Therefore, when this other kid did not want to pay me for selling his papers, I wanted to fight with him. Only I was too small to swing on this kid because he was much taller and about there years older than I was. Nevertheless, when he told me he was not going to pay I said, "Okay, if you are not going to pay, hit me with your best shot." The kid swung and I ducked, then I grabbed him around his legs and pulled him down. When he hit the ground, I started to hit him in the head. I was winning until the kid bit me on the arm. He bit me hard. I started to cry. It just so happened that my older brother, Bill — who was the same age as the kid I was fighting — came along.

He asked me why I was crying and I told him what had happened. Bill did not ask the other kid for the money, he just walked over and said, "Don't you ever touch my brother." Moreover, with that he hit the other kid harder than my Dad did the man in the bar. The other kid began to cry and he ran home. I stopped crying and forgot all about the seventy- five cents the kid owed me.

As I was sitting here in the dark, thinking about that, I started to think about the time I asked God into my life. It was sort of like the same thing. When I got down on my knees, I was crying, and when I asked God into my life, I said to Him, "God, if you're real, you're going to have to hit me over the head for me to believe you're real." I did not say, "Hit me with your best shot," but it was close enough. I was not depressed or beat by the system; I needed His help so I could help others. He was there for me and He told me what was to come the next day. I have been blessed more than I will ever deserve since that day.

So if you ever feel like telling someone, "Hit me with your best shot," ask Him to first. Ask Him from the heart or you are wasting your time. I know this because I asked Him four times before and received nothing. I was asking for myself, for my needs. However, when I told Him it was not for me but for others, from the heart, He was there for me. He has been there ever since. Man, I love Him so much.

"I love you, but I could never love you as much as He does."

Brother Bob

It's a Family Affair

Aloha, family, friends and all of God's children,

Do you remember all of those special times you had with your family? I remember a few. I recall, "Seeing" much more. I remember seeing my younger brother holding onto my father's finger. I remember going to the fair with the family. However, as I said, I remember more of "seeing" those things happen. That's because I came from a family of twelve children. It was hard growing up in a family that large. I felt that I was a black sheep in the family. Maybe my siblings felt that way, too, I do not know.

I never felt loved as a child. I felt like I was taken care of by someone.. (Strange how that felt.) One of my brothers, George, felt the same way. He seemed to be in trouble all the time. I even saw five of my other siblings and my mother gang up on him. They were swinging their fists at him left and right, and the girls were scratching him when they could. One of the older boys hit George, and as he was falling to the kitchen floor, he hit his head on the corner of the kitchen windowsill. It knocked him out.

They started to kick him when he was lying there on the floor. I cried and tried to stop them but they just pushed me away. George was thirteen and I was eight. I remember days like that more than I remember the good times. There were more bad times than good in those growing years. When I look at those pictures above, I think about being alone and crying by myself in a corner or sitting on the school playground by myself wishing I were dead.

When we grow up to be adults, we sometimes carry the old baggage with us. I did. It was not until I asked our Father in heaven to help me, when He took away all the pain and sadness of those days gone by, that

I was able to live. The picture of life as America sees it is just as you see it in the pictures above. However, real life does not start until you see life through God's eyes. Until or when you choose to see His way, you will not know what real life is all about. That is a fact. You will never know what you are missing until you ask Him for His help and His love. That is a fact. Are you listening, or are you just reading the words? If you feel anything at all in your heart right this very moment that is telling you to shout out for His love, "do it." He is knocking on your door.

"I love you, but I could never love you as much as He does."

Brother Bob

Dialogue

Aloha, family, friends, and all of God's children,

People like to hear themselves talk, I believe. All too often, that can become a very hazardous thing in one's life. We all need to listen more to those around us. If we did, we would not suffer as many of the repercussions that we do in life.

Take my relationship with the first girl I fell in love with, for example. I was twenty-two and she was eighteen. I had just come up to Seattle from California. I had nowhere to live, nor could I find the work I wanted to do down in California, so I came up to Seattle, where my family and friends lived. After living there for about four months, I decide to call a few women whose phone numbers I had in my wallet. I was drunk most of the time I met these women, so whenever I made a phone call to one of them, I had not a clue who they were.

When I came across Valerie's number, I remembered that she had a certain freshness about her. As I reflected on what I could remember, I thought about her sense of humor. She was so alive and eager to explore life. She was also very lovely with a very inviting body. As I reflected on her good qualities, I recall also that I did not see any negative things coming from her in conversation. I admired this in a woman, so I gave her a call. The problem was that I called her when I was drunk. At that age, I had no idea that I was an alcoholic yet.

It was about seven in the evening and I asked her if she and a friend would like to go out. I told her that my older brother, Jerry, was with me and that if she had a friend, she may feel more comfortable on this first date. What I did not tell Val is that I had a closed black eye, and the other I could hardly see from. (I had been in a bar fight two nights before. I wanted to see what it was like to get beat instead of winning. That is another story, however.) This gives you somewhat of an idea of what I was like in those years. I wasn't crazy, although I had been told I acted like it at times. It was more like an overload of testosterone.

Anyway, Val agreed to meet with us in one hour. She said she had a couple of roommates and one of them would come along. I told her my car had broken down so she would have to pick us up. It was a lie. I told a lot of lies in those days. I cannot look back and get depressed about those lying years. I am not where I am supposed to be yet, but I am not where I used to be, either. This is by the grace of God alone.

From that night on, we saw one another until seven years later. We were in love. The problem was that I had no idea what I wanted in life, so I spent most of my time drinking and raising hell. When I say "raising hell", by that I mean, letting Satan take control over my life, and letting evil prevail over good. Val loved me with all of her heart and soul. She was everything a man could want in a woman. Yet because of my need for drink and women, and because of my immaturity, I had not a chance of marrying her. I knew this, so I drank even more. I didn't care about life, as people in general did. I was a happy drunk, but I wouldn't hesitate to fight if the chance came along. The thing that I remember the most about Val and me in our relationship, was that our dialogue was one-sided.

"How could there be "dialogue" if it was one sided, Bob?" You might ask. I'm glad you asked; there was not any. That's my point. How many of you listen to your mate or your boss or your parents talking, but you return no dialogue? You sit there, listen and say, "Yeah, uh-huh, okay, you bet...," That is what I did. I would hear the voice, but my mind was not on the topic of discussion.

Many women will say we just do not have any communication anymore. Maybe two people will be talking and before one even finishes what they have to say, the other thinks they know the answer and voices it. Not only is that rude, but it infuriates your mate. You cannot sit and listen to someone, I mean really hear the words, and at the same time be thinking of what you are going to say before the other is finished speaking. Yet that is exactly what so many do. Not only does this happen in marriages, but in everyday conversation with others as well.

Why would this be of such a concern? Think about it: Have you ever become upset with someone when you are interrupted in mid-sentence. Sure, you have. You had something very important to tell someone you love but that person is not hearing a word you are saying. It is rude and upsetting to most all who have had it happen to them.

The point is that you must listen, and then think about what that person said, and then give an honest opinion. If I had heard the words of people who where trying to help me, I may have made changes in my life. However, if you are self-centered and egotistical, you need to change in order to save your marriage. Just as children must listen to learn, we to must listen to grow. We need to keep in touch with our feelings and share them with those we hold so close to our hearts. One way to do this is listening and hear their needs and wants.

Proverbs 18:13 says, "He who answers before listening, that is his folly and his shame." In addition, if you want to know more about your mate or others, know your heart and theirs. Proverbs 18:15 says, "The heart of the discerning acquires knowledge; the ears of the wise seek it out."

I hurt a woman who I felt I loved. I felt her pain when I was sober. I cried in shame for the hurt that I caused her. I learned something about myself after we parted: I learned that I would continue hurting others and myself until the day I quit drinking. Nevertheless, I also learned that I did not listen — or even care to listen — to those who wanted to love me. "Self-pity," indeed: try self-centered, immature, angry, and definitely, alone. I was all of these things and more. But by the grace of God, I now seek wisdom by hearing what is spoken and have found hope by faith.

I have made mistakes. However, even if it takes forty-five years, such as it did with me, it is never too late to ask for help. You know in your heart where the help is but you are afraid of losing yourself if you ask. Do not be. If you ask your Father for His help, you will find what it is you are here on earth to do. Doesn't that alone excite you?

I am not preaching, and I do not want you to think I am. I only want you to be all that you can be. To keep that someone special in your life, listen to her or him and find out for yourself what God has planned for the two of you. Listen to them and then listen to your heart. He is waiting for you to ask for His help. Listen to what He has to say, you will really enjoy life then.

"I love you, but I could never love you as much as He does."

Brother Bob

Bringing Back the Laughter

Aloha, family, friends, and all of God's children,

My wife is, most often, a happy person with a lot of joy to send around to those she meets or sees each day. However, today, she was sad and had tears because of her job situation. So I felt led to write this letter to her, to hopefully bring the real her back to our pet dog, Smoochie and me. Here is what I was led to say to her:

"Don't struggle with things you can't change,
Concentrate on the good things in your life,
Discontent can become nothing more than a bad habit — a costly attitude that can rob you of the pleasure of living."
Author Unknown

So, pick yourself up, honey and let's hit the waves: "surf's up!"

Apostle Paul said in Philippians 4:12, 13
"I know what it is to be in need,
I know what it is to have plenty,
I have learned the secret of being content in any and every situation, whether well fed or hungry, whether living in plenty or in want, I can do everything through Him who gives me strength."

"I love you, but I could never love you as much as He does".

Brother Bob

Contract Forms with God

Aloha, family, friends, and all of God's children,

Before I started to write these letters, I did not sign a contract with God. I did not say to Him, "Listen, buddy, if you let me do some writing and help me get it published, I'll do anything you say, up to a point."

I did not cut a deal to get my name in papers or my face on TV. However, I do want to share with you what I did say. I said, "God, if you're real, you're going to have to hit me over the head with a sledgehammer to get through to me." I said this because I had prayed so many times before and received nothing from Him that I thought He might not be real. I went to him for one reason only: to get Him to help me help the homeless, nothing else at all. My heart had been broken in so many ways the previous forty-five years that I must be strong enough and wise enough to help others get out of any mess they were in. (Not me, I, but God working in me.) As you have read already in this book, He answered my prayers. I had not a clue as to how powerful He is. It was amazing when He started to tell me why I had gone through everything that I had experienced. He was saying it was because I would need all of those lessons to help others. Man, was I shocked. No, it was more like......what is the word I am looking for here? It was as if I was in heaven here on earth. That is absolutely how it felt. Like God was right there inside of me. (He was, actually, by way of the Holy Spirit, but I would not learn what all of this meant for some time to come.) The feeling cannot be described. If you have heard a pastor, minister, or any kind of anointed saint talk about what it feels like to know God and Jesus, they will tell you, "You cannot put in words the feeling inside of how it feels." It is true; it is impossible. You have to experience it yourself or you will never know.

A young man in the Coast Guard once told me that he had just been saved and he was so excited. I just thought to myself, "Oh right, another wacko." However, at the same time, I thought to myself, "He sure seems to be excited about something that I think can't be so. Maybe there is something to this born-again Christian thing, after all." However, I was not ready to give up my life.

"What if it's not true and I just make a fool of myself? What if it is true and I can't do what I want if I give my life to God? What if it is true and I do not live up to God's expectations. I'm not ready for this kind of *%^@^ in my life right now!"

Those were some of the things going through my mind after I spoke to this young man. It is just amazing what it is all really about now that I look back at everything. It is like when I say to myself, "Boy, if I only knew then what I know now…," kind of statements. The only thing now that is different is that I am telling you as best I can what that young man was trying to tell me at that time. Will you listen? "Can you hear me now"? Will you take advantage of this book you are reading and make the most important change in your life?

What kind of contract can you make with God? No contract at all. You can try to make a deal and fill out the forms with Satan, if you wish. However, you had better believe me when I tell you that Satan is real and he will take advantage of you in a heartbeat. Remember what the Bible says is truth. Therefore, you had better believe that Satan is real. I know he is.

I didn't fill out a contract with Satan, but I did make the mistake of challenging him. I would have lost the fight, but I trusted God to pull me through it all the way. What I experienced in that battle I would not wish on my worst enemy, if I had one. There are some of you, reading this book right now, who are sitting in a very lonely place. It may be a park or a side street, or in a vacant house out in the sticks. It may be in your home that is so dirty and grungy that you would not want your worst enemy see it because you are so embarrassed by it. On the other hand, you may live in a vacant van or a beat-up car. Maybe you have a box that you sleep in. (Just like a dog in hiding.) I know those places because I slept in all of them myself. You wonder what happened to you. However, you are not alone.

There are those who have a home that has three or four bedrooms. It looks like the grand home you grew up in back when. Rich parents and grandparents who gave you whatever you wanted. Nevertheless, you are not happy living in it. Sure, it is nice, warm and comfortable. Nevertheless, your heart is about to explode.

It does not matter what kind of material place you live in or how much money you have if you are sad all the time. You may say, "I know all about that #*^+@. I don't want to hear it." However, you do need to hear it. You may have been told these words a thousand times, but you think you know it all and you do not want to hear it. "Bull...," you say. What have you done to make a change in your life if you think you know it everything? "Not a *%*#! thing." Right? You are not going to get out of the place you're in unless you do the one thing that will make you happy no matter where you live or how much money you have. You may get out of your troubles yourself, but it will not last very long. You will end up being unhappy again. You know I am right because it has happened before.

The difference between you making the change in your life versus God's way of change is this: even if you go from rags to riches or from rich to poor, you will always have peace in your heart, no matter where you are, because Jesus is with you. It is a fact, my brother and sister.

Listen: Millions of people do not walk in the Lord's path. Nevertheless, I can tell you a fact as sure as I know my name, those with Jesus in their heart can be happy no matter where they live or what they have. He is in the heart. That is what you get from God when you ask Him into your lives. That is why you see Christians smiling all the time; they have God's heart with in them. There is only one-way to do that and that is from your heart to His. Ask Him from the heart for help, not for your benefit alone but for others as well, and He will give you His heart. It is amazing, my friends, truly amazing.

Once you know what it is that He wants you to do, you will have a goal to reach that will be more exciting than life itself. You know, I still smoke cigarettes, and now and then, I use a cuss word or two. I am not perfect and neither is any other Christian. Nevertheless, we have heart. We have a desire to help others as much as we can and we hold every person dear to our hearts. Doesn't seem possible, does it? It's true, though. I still want to kick someone's butt now and then. I am an old soldier but I have found as time goes along that I would much rather give my love than get into a fight or in trouble. I am growing. I have become more and more mature.

You think you're mature. Not true. You do not know what that word means until He shows you how immature you have been acting all of these years. No offense intended here, my friend. I say these words to encourage you, not to hurt you. The fact is that we need to grow up. The world is filled with immature people. Everyone wants to be right. You see this in nations and countries around the world. You may say, "I can't make a difference." That is just you talking. God says we all can make a difference.

Even if you can help only one person for the rest of your life, that is someone who needed you and there was no one else who cared. You cared because God put this overwhelming love for others in your heart. You made a difference in that person's life. Once you do, you have been part of another person's reason to live. You are a hero. That is why we are all here. Not to be heroes but to love one another. When you go home to be with the Lord and He says to you, "I asked you to help just one person and you did as I asked. For this I am giving you the crown of love."

There may be another, who has helped thousands of people and God may say to this person, "I cannot give you the crown of love because you helped these people only to raise your own ego. For this I give you...,"

I mentioned to you that I sometimes cuss and that I still smoke. When I said that, something came to mind. I remember when I was coming back from Minnesota and I stopped in to see my brother in Seattle on my way back to Hawaii. Bill (my brother) and I went to have coffee in the early morning. I had been praying that one day God would help me to quit the cigarettes. I had been praying for this for a long time and I could not understand why He wouldn't take away the desire to smoke these nasty things. Well, Bill and I stopped at the 7-Eleven and I picked up a carton of cigarettes as well as my coffee. When we arrived back at my brother's home, I sat down to have my coffee and cigarettes. However, as I opened this fresh carton of smokes, I all of a sudden had no desire to smoke them. I knew, inside, that I would never want to have a cigarette again. I stopped that very moment and said to Bill, "I know you're not going to believe this but God just took away the desire to smoke any longer. Do you want this carton?"

Bill looked at me with what I thought was a look of something on the lines of, "This guy has really lost it."

Then he replied, "No, you better hold on to them. You may want one later."

I told him I was as sure of not wanting a cigarette again as I was when I said I would never want another drop of booze. I then told him I would give them to my brother Dennis when I arrived back in Honolulu. I did not have a cigarette, or the desire for one, for two years. After two years, I made the mistake of picking one up.

That old saying, "The devil made me do it," is more real than you know. Why would I have wanted to do that? I had not had the desire to smoke one cigarette for two years. Why did I have the need inside of me to have "just one"? I was tempted and I fell for it. I now smoke and have been again for almost five years now. I ask God to help me stop again but I think He is still teaching me a lesson. I do not know what it is, but I do know this: I was wrong for falling into temptation. The same thing goes for you that have a desire for alcohol or drugs. On the other hand, you lust for another woman other than your wife. You know it's wrong, but you want to please the flesh: big mistake!

I know what would happen if I picked up that bottle of booze? I would lose ten years of sobriety. That would be a huge mistake. I would be dead with in a year if I drank again. I know I would. However, more important than anything else is the realization that I would have hurt so many people. Not just God, but all of those who love me. I know some of you who are reading this have someone who loves you with all their heart, but you are not thinking of them, just yourself. Stop it. If you cannot or do not want to stop for yourself, stop for them and soon you will see that it was the right choice. If you think, you have no one who cares about you, think again: I do and so does God. I have said many times before, "There is something good about everyone here on earth." He or she just needs to know one thing: God loves you and wants you to come to Him for whatever it is you need. In addition, you do not need to make a contract with Him.

Think about it, and always remember:

"I love you, but I could never love you as much as He does."

Brother Bob and Jesus

A Sad Clown

Aloha, family, friends, and all of God's children,

Many can remember the days when they were children and they saw a clown for the first time. I do, anyway. It was at a circus in the small town I grew up in, New Rockford, NorthDakota. Just as every child does, I laughed; he was funny, and I thought how much fun it would be to make people laugh. My desire to make people laugh stayed with me up to this day. I have had a few of my friends tell me I should be a comic of some kind. My wife suggested this only a few days ago, in fact. So I thought about it and my conclusion is that if were I to be a stand-up comic, I would do a routine on being a homeless alcoholic. Many jokes would be true-life experiences that happened. The joke was not funny then, but funny now that I look back at them.

While watching the morning Christian channel today, one of the ministers told this joke: "The police were called to a condo building in downtown New York. They were told that two alcoholic men lived in unit number 2010 and that one of them had jumped out of the window. The police, upon entering into the unit up on the twentieth floor, saw a man standing by the window. The police officer asked the man (who was drunk) if he knew the person who jumped out. The man said he was a good friend of the jumper so the police asked him why he jumped. The alcoholic said that his friend thought he could fly around the building. So one of the officers asked the alcoholic why he didn't try to stop his friend from jumping out and his friend replied, 'I thought he could, too.'"

Being a former alcoholic, I know all too well that there is more truth to that joke than is known to many. I believe that I could tell many stories that would floor people in the audience, if I had the wish to do so, about my life as a homeless alcoholic and drug user. However, because of seeing much more sadness than joy while I was on the streets, I have been blessed to try to help these people instead of laughing about them. I can look back and laugh at myself now and then. I can even tell a couple of stories about myself that would be ok in God's eyes, but I could never make jokes about those who I know suffered just to better my own life with monetary benefits. I would be a hypocrite. To reach out and give a hand up to them, then turn around and joke about their sorrows and misgivings would be disgusting. (I say, "Hand up" because I will talk to them about "looking up" and going forward. It cannot be a "hand out" because many of these men and women I met out there would not take a "hand out" because of pride. I saw first hand that those who did not keep their pride would lose their will to live, which, of course, would eventually lead to their death. It happened more often than not.)

At one time, in my teenage days, my friends and I would call someone a "clown" if he did something stupid or took advantage of another. It was like an insult or, a "cut down" of that person, as we called it, to the other person. (One of my brothers used to say it to me often. He did not know it at the time, but I would be a clown to him just to make him mad. He is an older brother, so I liked to get under his skin whenever I could. However, when I was on the streets, I would try to humor others just to ease the pressure of everyday life. I was a happy drunk, on the outside, but on the inside, I was very confused with the world and all who walked it. I would tell jokes and be a friend, but I had no one who I could trust to confide in. Needless to say, I was probably the saddest clown on the street.

I had to find out what my responsibilities were to society and myself. It took thirteen years on the streets before I came to the Lord and I have learned much since those days. One of the things that I learned is that it is our responsibility to believe in His ability.

I watched TV this week to see a very great person, a child of God, being praised for all that he did for our country. President Ronald Reagan believed in our Lord and he was not afraid to tell of his love. Now that he is gone, I see those in the news media saying cruel things and very distasteful comments. What the news media does is one of the things that used to anger me in my days of old. To me, the newspaper is just another form of gossip for many who write in it. It would anger me so much that I would go out and get drunk. "Stinken' thinken". As I read the paper today and see what was written, I pray for those who hurt others. Just as the president did when he was shot, he prayed for the man who shot him. We have to pray for those who hurt others. How can we not?

Ruth (my wife) told me that I remind her of President Reagan in some ways. I asked why, and she said, "You bothhave so much faith in God and have so many of the same principles." This took me by surprise because I thought the only thing she noticed about me was my desire to fish all the time. (Just kidding, I joke about myself when I am trying to be humble.) Her comment made me think of those days on the streets. How I thought nothing was worthliving for. By asking God for His help, I was graced with being able to sit and see a wonderful child of God receiving all the praise he well deserved because of God's grace upon him.

I am not the man I used to be, but I am not where I should be, yet. We change every day. With out change, we would have a boring life. As an alcoholic, I had no daily changes: I just got drunk. This was a downhill motion. However, because I asked God to change me, I see daily how I can help others to change for the betterment of self and mankind. I saw another sermon on the television where the pastor said there are seven deadly sins that we do not think about. He suggested that we look in the mirror and ask ourselves if we have these sins in our lives. In addition, if we do, pray for change to come about.

They are:

1. Laziness
2. Gluttony
3. Greed
4. Lust
5. Envy
6. Anger
7. Pride

If we take a good honest look at ourselves, and we see these things controlling our lives, we need to change. It is possible.

> *"And God will meet all your needs according to his glorious riches in Christ Jesus."*
>
> Philippians 4:19

A psychologist once said this in an interview when asked what the one thing people fear the most was. "There are actually two things that people fear in life. One is the fear of death. And the other is the fear of change." I believe we should fear neither. I look forward to one with extreme joy in my heart and live with excitement for the other, not knowing what the day will bring. That bothare for my betterment, by His grace, are more than I could ask for. My, my, my, what will tomorrow bring? What an exciting thought that is.

This clown is no longer a sad clown. Today, I will be joyful in His love. What could bring more happiness than that, I ask you.

"I love you, but I could never love you as much as He does."

Brother Bob

Crackers and Milk

Aloha, family, friends, and all of God's children,

The movie, Fried Green Tomatoes, dealt with friendship, pain, and sorrow. The only thing that movie was missing was crackers and milk. I thought a movie with a title like that must have people in it who eat crackers and milk. I remember that when I first told my wife that I was going to have a bowl of crackers and milk, she laughed.

I asked her why that was funny and she said, "You aren't serious, are you?"

I thought everyone had crackers and milk when they were growing up. (Maybe they only eat them in NorthDakota.) Then there would be huge kettles of rice quite often, as well. Milk and rice, with a little cinnamon on it, was the best meal a kid could ask for. Maybe not: I sure liked those big kettles of oatmeal in the morning.

"What do crackers and milk have to do with me taking up my time to read this letter, Bob?"

Thank you. I'm glad you asked that question. When I was watching Joyce Meyer on the picture tube this morning, one of the things she talked about was (no, not crackers and milk…) the difference between "giving" and "to give." As Joyce was explaining the difference between the two, I thought about my mother's giving. Some of us children were sitting and having some crackers and milk one day when there was a knock at the back door. It was a man who lived behind our house, some distance away. When Mother saw him, she went to the refrigerator, took out a big bowl of cooked food and gave it to him. I asked her why she helped him and Mother said, "It's always better to give than to receive."

His nickname was "Bimbo," and he rode around town on a little old tractor, a very old tractor. I didn't know it at the time, but Bimbo was an alcoholic and he had had a stroke at one time. Therefore, when he walked, he had a limp on his left side and his left arm hung down to the side. I suppose that that little tractor was all he was able to drive. I do not know this for sure, but he did not appear to have a job.

Bimbo lived behind our house. We had a very large piece of property, so to me it was a long walk across that field. However, Bimbo would. He would come by and ask for food, and unbelievably, we had leftovers for him, even though there were twelve children.

My friends and I used to go to Bimbo's little trailer house and knock on his windows at night. He would get mad and come outside and we would run. We knew he couldn't catch us, so we would laugh and tease him. One day, Mother asked me if we were going over to Bimbo's and bothering him. We said we had done that a couple of times and she put a stop to that quickly. Therefore, we did the next best thing: When Bimbo drove his tractor down the street, we would sing a song that was popular at that time, "Bimbo, Bimbo, whatchya going to do-ie-o." He would pick something up from his little box he had behind him and throw it at us until someone on the street would chase us off.

Again, Mother asked us, "Are you kids bothering Bimbo again?" We lied and said no. She looked at us with that stern look and said, "I know you were, because someone called and told me all about it." (You cannot get away with anything in Mayberry. That goofy Deputy Barney probably called and told, I thought to myself.) Then Mother told us to go in the closet. (Dennis, my kid brother, was with me.)

We hated the closet. Once we were inside, we heard Mother put the knife in the door in place of a lock. Sometimes it seemed as if we had been staying in there for hours. So it seemed to us. Sometimes we would just cry ourselves to sleep. At times, I would grab the handle of the door and shake the door until the knife dropped out. If I was lucky, Mother would not hear the knife hit the floor and I would sneak out. However, when I came back, I would be in even bigger trouble.

One time after Dennis and I slipped out of the closet, we had to come back in and face the music. When we walked in, Mother was shocked. She said, "How did you little brats get out with out me seeing you?" It was more of a question to herself than it was to us. She then told me to go and get her belt. Therefore, I went into her room and I picked up her dress belt that was paper-thin. When she saw the belt, she said, "This isn't the belt that I meant." Nevertheless, she let it go at that. She then told us to drop our pants and bend over. We did as we were told and as we did, I whispered to Dennis, "Pretend that you're hurt and start crying when she hits us."

When Mother hit us, we begin to yell as if we were struck with a whip. She started to smile after the third swing because she knew we were trying to fool her. She must have thought we had really overdone our act, because before long she was laughing hysterically.

She said, "Oh, you boys aren't hurt that bad. This belt is like a piece of paper." Nevertheless, she thought it was so cute that she just told us to go upstairs to our rooms. When we reached the top of the stairs, we laughed so hard we thought we would wet our pants.

As my thoughts went back to Joyce Meyer, she was now talking about staying focused and she used the audience as an example. She was right about how, we viewers — and those who were in the church — would drift off thinking about something else while she spoke. Be it shopping when they leave the church or what to make for dinner, etc, etc. I had drifted off thinking about Bimbo,however, not before I heard the full sermon about giving. Joyce had said that "to give" meant nothing more than to give someone a cup of coffee or to give someone your advice. However, in "giving," you are giving from the heart. You feel good when you are giving your time to help others or you are giving someone food so that they may be healthier.

That is what Mother was doing when she was giving food to Bimbo. Mother felt in her heart the need to give someone not as fortunate as we were. Even though, we were poor in our little town, Mother would still have it in her heart to be giving to others. I, even at that young age, saw what she was doing and knew it was a good thing to do. Today, I look back at those days and I think how valuable her lesson was to us. We were taught to help those in need. I was blessed to have such a mother.

Mother's kindness rubbed off on each one of her children. My brothers and sisters would not hesitate for a moment, to help someone in need. As you will see in letters to come, not only did I learn from

Mother's kindness, I would also find out where she received so much love to share.

The next time I have a bowl of crackers and milk, I will no doubt think about the lesson I learned at a young age: the joy of giving.

"I love you, but I could never love you as much as He does."

Brother Bob

A Miracle or Just Dumb Luck?

Aloha family, friends and all of God's children,

How often have you heard someone say, "It's a miracle," or "It was just dumb luck"? Others may say, "It's an answer to prayer."

In the dictionary, it says this about miracles: "A supernatural event as due to divine action, e.g."

Look up the word, "luck," in the dictionary and it says something like, "Chance/ good fortune/success due to chance/the tendency of a person to be persistently fortunate or unfortunate as luck would have it, fortunately/ unfortunately, to be down on one's luck esp. in some specified set of circumstances: to try one's luck to take a chance, esp. in gambling."

Therefore, here is my question: "Do you feel lucky"? "Well, do you, punk?" (Everyone who went to see Clint Eastwood's movie in which he said those words should find the humor here.) If, in real life, those words were spoken to someone with a gun pointed at their head I would be willing to guess that the person at the other end of that gun barrel would be praying. When a person is in a very difficult situation, he or she, in most all cases, would ask God for help and not count on their luck. They would pray, not rub a rabbit's foot or some other so-called, "good luck charm." Yet, when the name Jesus comes up in a conversation, the person listening will find some reason to change the subject or will come up with an excuse to walk away from the conversation all together. Go figure.

In real life, people pray in church but many pray behind closed doors. They ask God for His help, God responds with all of His love, and your prayer is answered. Yet, you do not want to go around and tell everyone about how He helped you. Why? I will tell you why. People have been programmed over the years by television, newspapers, your peers, and reading material that Christians are a bunch of weak and greedy people. If you are a Christian, please do not be offended. I was like that, too. I thought that when a Christian walked up to me and started to talk about God, that he or she was a weak person. They had no answer of their own so they went to this false God. However, 98 percent of the American people believe there is a "higher power." When I asked God to come into my life, I was not in a life-or-deathsituation: I wanted His help so that I could help others.

Let me tell you how God helped me when I asked Him for His help,

1. I had a slipped disk in my neck and I was told that I needed a laser operation.
2. I had torn cartilage in my right knee and I was told that I needed an operation.
3. I had a torn muscle in my right shoulder and I was told that I needed an operation.
4. I was told I was an Alcoholic and that I would be all my life.
5. I was told from my early days of life, as far back as I can remember, that I would never amount to anything.
6. I was led by society to believe that people who believed in God were weak and unstable.
7. I was told that I would never live past forty-five years of age.

When I asked God to forgive me of my sins, He did. In addition, He gave me much, much more. I cannot in any way, explain to you how He works in a way that will make you believe that God really does answer prayers and does miracles, every day.

However, I can tell you the truth about what He has done for me: He has healed me of all my pains that are mentioned above. I have had no operations and I have not gone out to bars and become falling-down drunk. I do not drink at all. I am fifty-six years young, not forty-five. I know there is a God, and Jesus died for our sins. Moreover, by the grace of God, I believe that one day I will be an evangelist traveling around the world spreading His word. These things were/are made possible by God alone.

Listen, some of you folks who receive my letters may be saying to yourselves, "Why doesn't Brother Bob quote scripture more"?

My answer to this question is this, "I am led by the Holy Spirit to speak as He wishes for me to speak. I am what I like to call, "for real." In other words, I tell you how I feel from the heart. God allows me to do this. If you have a question, you need to go to the Word for the answer. He has every answer in the Word. I do not remember the last time I asked a pastor a question about God or Jesus; I go to the Bible. I will ask my pastor his opinion on certain matters and I know that I will be grateful for his wisdom. Ultimately, God is the source of all the answers concerning Him. He has the answer to where, what, how, and when, to do all that you do. He wants you to know Him and there is no better way than reading the Word for yourself. I go to church and I am grateful to learn much from my Pastor. Nevertheless, you learn more firsthand. Just as you learn by example, you learn by studying. Praise God.

Therefore, the next time you feel "lucky," think about what luck really is. There is no such thing as "luck." He has a reason for everything. You may not see it or know it, but He has all the answers you need. If you really want to know what life is all about, why luck has nothing to do with your life, ask Him from the heart. You will see that all that society has taught you was wrong when it comes to knowing who and what Christians are really all about. You must remember that they only want the best for everyone and they are learning, just as you are. However, they are learning how to do it the right way — God's way — not man's. No one is perfect. However, you, I, and everyone else should always be open to listening to others. If nothing else, it is just courteous to do so.

The next time someone says to you, "Go ahead; make my day," say to him or her, "God really loves you."

"I love you, but I can never love you much as He does."

Brother Bob

The ABCs of Life

Aloha, family, friends and all of God's children,

"You know, you are really ignorant, Dennis!"

As soon as I said this to my brother, I knew he was going to take it the wrong way. I could almost feel his anger on the other end of the phone. He was steaming, I was sure, and it became clear in his tone of voice.

"What the hell are you talking about? Now, I'm ignorant, huh?" Dennis replied.

"Dennis, I didn't mean that the way it came out," I said, as I almost bit my tongue for not choosing the right words. "What I mean is this: You say you have read the Bible, but to me, it's clear that you do not understand anything that you've read. Anyone can read the Bible or any other book. But, if you or I just read it and we have no one to ask what we are reading means, we are really 'ignorant' of anything our mind is taking in. That is why we have teachers. Each of us has to let our ego lie back in the corner of our mind and listen to someone who knows what he or she is talking about. You can read the Bible and still be ignorant about what it means, just as I am ignorant about the mechanics of an air-conditioning system. You know everything there is to know about an air conditioner, Dennis, because you studied about it and someone taught you what the manual meant."

Dennis already knew the things I spoke of. What I believe he was really doing was looking for an argument as to why I think all the things you read in the Bible are true. I will not argue with him or anyone else. No one is going to believe anything I say if their mind is set to believe what they want to believe anyway. You may be reading things that are false about creation. However, you believe those books because of your ignorance of the Bible.

"Dennis," I said, "I think that people should go and talk to God to find the answers they seek."

I knew that this statement to Dennis would bring a laugh out of him, and it did. We went on talking a little more, but our conversation ended the same way as it usually does when we speak about our Lord: with both of us a little more concerned about the other.

Dennis and I are not only brothers, but we are also best friends. That is how I see us anyway. One time, I introduced Dennis to someone I knew as my friend. As we parted from this person, Dennis said to me, "Why did you introduce me as your friend?" With out waiting for an answer, he said, "That was a real insult to me. Are you too embarrassed to introduce me as your brother or are you just too ashamed of me?"

I was surprised by the feeling he had. "No, no! Not at all! That was a compliment to you, Dennis. How many people can say that his brother is also his friend? I did not intend to hurt your feelings at all, Dennis. That is the last thing I would ever do to you or anyone else in our family. Heck, no! I don't want that to happen."

I could understand why he felt that way, though, because Dennis and I have been close since birth. He is one year younger than I am, and when we were growing up, we spent all of our time with one another. When we were in high school, we started to drift apart because I started to get stupid on the booze. Then, when I came back from Vietnam, it became a little worse because I started to drink more. He tried so hard to be a good brother to me over the years. I mean, no one on this earth could ask for a better brother than I have in my brother, Dennis. When I was delivered from alcohol, Dennis and I could argue, with out having to worry about losing a brother because of our difference of opinion. I am blessed, and am grateful to God for keeping Dennis in my life to share these last years together with me. I am grateful beyond words. God bless you, Dennis, "my friend". ;-)

This letter is going to be a little longer than the others are. That is because I cannot talk about what God told me this morning in a short time. He wants me to tell you that life is not as hard as you think it is. It is difficult at times, yes, but it is not difficult all the time. That is to say, it is only hard if you let it be. The way to peace is through the word of God. Again, to those of you who think that I am preaching, I am not. I want you to hear something that I have learned. They are not my words, but God's. You have to be open to what I say or you're going to miss the big picture. God told me to talk to you as if I were talking to one of my best friends, such as Dennis. The only thing is that you have to be open-minded and willing to learn the truth and not something you read out of a fictional book like The Da Vinci Code.

I did not think it was possible to believe there was a God until He spoke to me audibly. However, when He did, He showed me that life is very simple if you trust in Him. That's all you have to do. Once you do, you will want to know more and more about the Bible, and how it proves itself true. I recommend the book, The Bible: Fact or Fiction? by Dr. Witty. The Bible truly does prove itself. You have to have someone teach you the basics of it and read about how it is proven that all that the Bible says is true. I have nothing to gain by lying to you about this. I have nothing to gain by telling you how to get wisdom, or to grow in this life of ours with knowledge of all there is to know "about life". You have to want to know the truth. Once you do, you will find that what it says in the Bible is true: "The truth shall set you free" (John 8:32).

I would like to tell you something that is personal and meaningful to me. I once took care of a couple named Sue and Don who lived on the Big Island of Hawaii. They had moved to Hawaii from Italy. They are in their sixties or early seventies, I believe. Although it was a very short job, I never could have imagined that what was to happen that would affect all three of us for a very long time.

I was their house cleaner, gardener, maintenance man, and chauffeur. I had planned to have my wife be part of the job, but that did not work out. I was trying to do it all by myself, and that is why it did not work out. However, what happened one night is what I believe was the reason God put us on the same path at the right time.

I had just finished my job and I went home for the night. I was using their car because I would be taking Sue to the beach in the morning. About 2:00 am, the phone rang. When I answered it, I was surprised to hear Don's voice on the other end.

He said, "Bob, Sue is in really bad shape. I think I need to get her to the hospital as soon as I can. I think it will take the ambulance too long to get here. Do you think you can get her to the hospital on time?"

I knew in my heart that this was very serious indeed. I replied, "Don, I know the ambulance can't get there before I do. I can be there in less then ten minutes and we will be at the hospital with in the hour." We lived about seven miles away from each other. It takes me, on a normal drive, about fifteen to eighteen minutes to get to their house. The road to their home is windy, narrow, dark, and dangerous if you did not know the road.

I ran to the car, and with each step I was saying, "God, please let me get over there in time and get Sue to the hospital." I thanked Him for allowing me to be there for them in a time of need. I thanked Him for making sure that the hospital would be ready to take her into emergency and that the doctors were on hand to fix the problem or problems.

When I arrived at the house, Don was shocked that I got there so quickly. I found out later that I made it in less then ten minutes. We had to now drive another fifty-five miles of very windy roads. This drive normally takes me fifty minutes, at the least. We arrived at the hospital in twenty minutes. They rushed her into the emergency room and Don told me that I should go home and he would call me as soon as he heard anything.

It took about ten hours before Don called me back to give me the news. I had been waiting by the phone because I knew he would need me no matter what the outcome was. When I picked up the phone, Don's voice was hard to understand. It sounded as if he were crying. I felt that even though he was crying that somehow it was good news.

Don said, "Bob, the doctors just came out and told me Sue is going to be just fine. They had to do an operation on her and she came out all right. She will have to be here for a while and I am going to stay with her. They are going to bring in a bed for me to sleep on. Bob, they said that if we had not been here at just the right time, she would have died. They said that if it had been even five minutes longer, she would not have made it at all. Thank you for getting Sue to the hospital so quickly. I know the ambulance couldn't have gotten her here as fast as you did." Then, he started to cry loudly.

After a few moments, I said, "Don, it wasn't me at all that did this for your wife; it was the Lord." He was still crying and I was not sure if he heard what I had said.

Then he replied, "It had to be the Lord, Bob, because she is still alive."

I told him that he did not need to worry about the house or anything at all. I told him to rest and when Sue gets better, I will come to see her.

When I went to the hospital and walked in with a bouquet of flowers, Sue looked up at me and stretched out her arms. I walked over and hugged her. With tears in her eyes, she said, "Thank you, Bob, for saving my life."

I smiled and whispered in her ear, "It was God, our Father, Sue." With that, she began to sob.

What I did not tell you in this story so far is that these people were very aristocratic. They have a mansion on a hill that overlooks the ocean and all of the best hotels on the Big Island of Hawaii. In their study, they have portraits of family members back in Italy. They look like dukes, duchesses, and lords. Sue once told me that they knew the Pope personally.

On another wall are pictures of a prince from Saudi Arabia and one of Sidney Poitier. Other pictures of movie stars and more people of nobility hung on the wall as well. Sue and Don were not your ordinary neighbors. When my wife, Ruth, and I first met them, I had sensed that there was something special about them. I had no idea how important they were until one day; Sue said to me, "Bob, why don't you and Ruth come over to Italy for the next Olympics in Greece. We will pay for everything and I will introduce you to some very important people. You will love it in Italy. Did I tell you that the Pope came to our home and blessed it for us?"

I said no, she had not, and I wondered if she could see the amazement on my face. She said that they were very devout Catholics and that God had been very good to them. The reason I am telling you this now is that when I first met them, our relationship was one of, "the upper class with the servants." However, when we parted ways, it was one of friendship and love for one another.

The ABCs of it is this: "You cannot ever, ever imagine what God has planned for you in the coming days ahead." That is what life is about. The ABCs of it all is that life is not always easy, but if we let God guide us instead of us trying to figure out what tomorrow may bring, we will do just fine.

It took me to many years to see that my pain and worry was for nothing. Today, I am most happy because things that happen, like meeting Sue and Don, could never have had the outcome that they did had it not been for God's love for each of us.

With that, I say this:

"I love you, but I could never love you as much as He does."

Brother Bob

Two Brothers Fishing

4/24/04

Aloha, my friends, family and all of God's children,

While watching the movie Good Will Hunting on TV, I realized the genius of the script. There was a time in my life when I would not have understood that movie. I was quite taken aback by the realization of the fact that when I was drinking, I really had not understood what life was all about. That is to say, when I was sober during my drinking days, I thought I was going along, day-by-day, fully aware of my surroundings. Today, I came to the obvious understanding: obvious now that I've been sober for nine years, that my brain was slowly deteriorating one day at a time.

Since I have been living life one day at a time sober, my mind now comprehends words, actions, scenes, etc., with not only my eyes wide open but my heart as well. I may be assuming, but a doctor or a psychologist may say these are normal occurrences of the mind rejuvenating itself because of the new method of living. On the other hand, one may say that I have grown up and am taking responsibility for my actions since I have given up the bottle. "Nay," I say to all. It is my belief, with all the heart and soul from with in, to tell you it is the wisdom of God and His forgiveness.

One does not have to be an alcoholic, a drug addict, or a formerly institutionalized patient to know when God has blessed them. You only have to ask Him to open your eyes and your heart to the world to gain the wisdom that I have learned. My, what an exciting day this has become.

Let me tell you a story from the heart: I once was going on a fishing trip with my one of my older brothers in Seattle, Washington. The salmon were running at the time, so there were many to be caught. I was excited about this trip for two reasons, even if it was to be for only one day. One reason was the chase to catch a twenty- or thirty-pound salmon, and the other was the opportunity to fish with Bill. Bill is three years older than I am, so I respected him just as I had taught myself to respect anyone older than myself. However, Bill never let me forget that he was the older brother. (Anyone who has an older brother understands what I mean by saying that.) Bill and I never spent much time together because I was an alcoholic and Bill never knew if I was going to be "the good guy" or "the bad guy" on any given day.

As we were going out over the waves of Puget Sound this very wet and windy day, we were soaked from head to foot. However, I was overwhelmed with joy. Each time we hit a wave, I would yell like a little kid with his first puppy. It was hard to hear one another because of the noise from the motor, the wind, and the rain. Then I heard Bill yell and did not understand him until the third yell, when he said, "Bobby, do you know what those mountains over there are called?" As he pointed at the Cascade Mountains. I, at first, was taken back by this question. I had lived in Seattle for twelve years!

"Why wouldn't I?" I asked myself. I did not think he asked me that because he thought I was stupid. The only other reason he had was to see if I had all of my faculties working. Therefore, showing respect, I yelled back, "The Cascades."

Then I went a little further and said, "Isn't this just the greatest?"

Bill yelled back, "What's that?"

I yelled back, "This is all God's, but He's sharing it with us. Isn't that great?"

I could tell he saw that I was speaking (rather, yelling) from the heart. For a moment there, I could see "his heart" in his eyes. He grinned a huge grin and nodded his head. He must have thought that I had all of my faculties together if I knew there was a higher power.;-)

In the movie, Good Will Hunting, Will, the star of the movie, was asked this question: "What would you like to do for the rest of your life"? Will had no answer. He had an answer to any question you may ask him, but no answer to that one. Here was a genius who had no answer to the one question that would guide his life. I had to ask myself this question: "More importantly, what would God want you to do?"

I don't know if it was the anger in my childhood, the alcohol, or the immaturity that kept me in the dark for forty-five years, but there is one thing I'm sure of and that is that I know, that I know, that I know, my wisdom and the dramatic change in my life was "not of me."

"What do you want to do in your life?" you might ask me. I will tell you, with a sure and sound heart: "I want to do what pleases my Father." He is a sure thing. He is the only directional course of hope. He is the answer.

"I love you, but I could never love you as much as He does."

Brother Bob

Questioning My Direction

Aloha, Family, Friends, and all of God's Children,

I recently wrote a letter to Ted Platt of Son Shine Ministries. Brother Ted is the partner of Reverend Lew at the ministry. They started Son Shine Ministry together. It would do your heart good to read some of Reverend Lew's works and to hear a few of his tapes. These two children of God are blessed indeed and I am grateful to know them personally.

I asked Ted four things in a letter that I sent to him: I asked about my inadequacy; I asked him about the fear of leaving my mother behind at her age and health. (Mother is eighty-seven and has suffered from a stroke. We are very close); I asked about being an evangelist; and I asked what he thought about me comparing myself with others.

Looking back at the time I wrote to Ted, I felt I needed his wisdom. After Pastor Lew had his stroke, it became almost impossible for him to write a letter. The pastor writes to me but it is of few words. I meant no disrespect to Pastor Lew, I just wanted to reach out to a child of God who could send me what they believed was God's answer to my questions in a detailed way. What follows is the letter I received from Brother Ted. Following his letter is my response to him.

I hope and pray that Ted's letter somehow helps you with some questions you may have. In addition, I pray that by you reading this, you find happiness in what you are doing and in what you have been blessed with. I know I have.

"I love you, but I could never love you as much as He does."

Brother Bob

Ted Platt, Letter and Reply

Son Shine Ministries International, Inc.
Post Office Box 456 • Azle, Texas • 76098-0456 • U.S.A.
Tel. 817-444-3777 • Fax 817-270-0199

May 25, 2005

Dear Bob,

Thank you for your letter and your generous gift to Son Shine Ministries. You are a faithful man of God. I can tell by your letter. It is obvious that you have a deep burden for souls. I understand how you feel. I will offer what the Lord has given me to share with you. Please take what I say to Jesus for His words to you concerning what I have shared.

First: your feeling of inadequacy. I have been there many times in the past, especially after Lew had his stroke. I considered Lew to be the most powerful Christian preacher and teacher I had ever heard. Souls were saved everywhere he went. After his stroke, I was the only one available to take over the preaching and teaching of the Christian Home Seminar. I felt so inadequate, but when I got up to speak, Jesus took over and did what He wanted to do. Many times, I hesitated to go, but as Jesus gave the strength and power, I went and He did great things. We are all inadequate in ourselves. Only Jesus working through us is what counts. I have never gotten up to speak that I wasn't nervous. But it went away as soon as Jesus took over.

Secondly, I believe your " fear" of leaving your mother is divinely inspired. I believe God wants you to care for her. It is scriptural. She needs you. Is she saved? If so, you can minister to her to not fear death, but that Jesus is waiting for her and at the proper time will call her home. Read the Bible to her. If she is not saved, this is a perfect opportunity to be an evange-

list and lead your mother to the Lord. For the last two years, we have taken care of our widowed son-in-law who had terminal cancer. He lived in our living room of our mobile home. He was saved so Barbara and I were able to minister to him not to fear death. We read the Bible to him and encouraged him in many ways. My sister was caring for our mother when she became terminally ill. We spent the last week of her life with her, ministering Jesus to her. She was so happy to be going home to be with Him.

Thirdly, there are many ways to be an evangelist. Speaking in front of a group is only one way. I believe the most powerful way in one-on-one with another person. I believe Jesus will give you many opportunities to minister salvation while you are caring for your mother. I had many opportunities to minister to my brother and sister and other family members during that week, many of whom I believe are not saved. Other ways of being an evangelist is by your example and through letters, books and song. I believe your "songs for the children" has ministered more than you realize. So be encouraged, Bob.

Jesus is the answer. Pray about everything.

Fourthly, I believe that comparing myself with other Christians is a waste of time. We all have spiritual gifts and each one of us is a vital part of the Body of Christ. Some get a great deal of visibility as they speak to large groups and others are hardly even noticed as they go about the work to which God has called them. You are a vital part of God's work wherever He puts you and what ever He has you doing.

Finally, let Jesus speak to you about these things I have shared. He may give you something completely different or may have you agree with all or part of this.

I pray this has helped. We love you and Ruth and would love to see you some day. Keep your eyes on Jesus and keep loving Him.

In Jesus' Name,

Ted Platt

Dear Ted,

"Much Mahalo", for your words of encouragement and wisdom. I have prayed on them and have been blessed with what I feel is the answer I have been searching for. Thank you also for the book. I had one copy already. I gave your copy to a brother I have visiting here from Montana. He has already read it once and is now going through it a second time. God Bless him and you.

This is what I feel the Lord has said: I will one day go across the U.S.A. and give my testimony.

I will send an introductory film and a copy of my book to each church I feel the Lord is directing me to call upon before I go. In the film, I will speak about raising money to buy more copies of my book to give to the homeless. I will also ask them if I can work for them in order to raise enough money to get to the next destination.

I will do as it says in 2 Thess. 3:10: "If anyone isn't willing to work, he should not eat."

I feel I have been graced with much of our Father's love and He will surely guide me on my path. As I wear His suit of armor, I will do my best to honor Him.

However, I cannot do these things for a while. For now, I shall do my tasks here and now. My sister is moving to Arizona, so I must stay and take care of Mother. When the time is right, I will go forth as He guides me on the mainland. Then one day, He will take me from nation to nation, as He had told me He would on the day He graced me with His words audibly.

You asked me if Mother was saved. That she is, indeed. In fact, she was saved a short time after me. I had told her of what God has said to me and what He had planned. She listened and as far as I could tell, believed in everything that I had said. A short time later, she went to a church with two of her friends from Seattle that lives here in Honolulu at times. At the end of that day, I had called her and she said that she had been saved. I was so excited for her. She now talks openly and freely about her faith and how much she loves the Lord for all He has done for her.

About two years after Mother had been saved I went to visit her at her home. As we sat talking about the Lord, I, for no reason, asked her if she thought that I would ever drink again. At which time, she looked me in the eye and she said, "You know, Bobby, I asked God that one day."

After she said just those few words, I could see her eyes start to get moist.

Then, she looked at me again and said, "When I asked God that question, Bobby, He said you would never touch alcohol again. It was such a strange feeling because my whole body and my whole mind knew that it was true." She began to get excited, and she wiped the tears from her checks. She then said, "I always knew that someday you would change but I didn't know that God was going to do it." At that moment, she began to sob.

I went to her and kneeled by her side, and I told her, "Mom, He always tells us the truth. I know, too, that I will never be a drunk again and I know that I will help all the people He said I would. Thank you, Mom, for always having faith in me and for praying for me all these years."

As the tears flowed, she said, "I did, too! I prayed for you kids every day. I didn't know then what it meant to be born again but I knew He was listening to me. Look at how all you kids turned out so good after having to go through what you did with your dad's drinking." She cried more. I soon had her laughing about all the silly things that we children did when we were young and she and I had a grand few hours together sharing our love.

Now, wasn't that a long answer to your question? (Sometimes I get carried away, but I love telling of God's love and His grace.)

When you said to me, "I believe your 'fear' of leaving your mother is divinely inspired," I thought, "You are correct." I will tell you why. (Uh oh, another long story.)

I once asked our Father, "Father, I wish to take care of my mother. I wish for you to keep her with us until she can see the results of your works concerning these things you have told me. I wish for her to come home to you, knowing that all of her children will be just fine when she leaves us. I will not be angry or childish about my not being able to do what it is that, "I want to do". I will listen and do as you say. But please, let Mother see what you have done with me. In Jesus's name. Amen."

You see, my prayer has been answered. Jesus has shown this to me through His love bestowed upon you and you shared His answer with me. I truly am where I should be at this time. Thank you, sir, and thank you, Father, who tells us all the truth.

Ruth read your letter and said, "Bob, this is really powerful. Who is Ted, again?" And so I once again told of you and Reverend Lew and Son Shine Ministries. She knew, of course, but it gave me reason again to boast of my love for you and Reverend Lew. God has blessed me in many, many ways, my brother. I have much that He wishes for me to do. I, at times, can barely stand the amount of love I have for Jesus and what He did for us. At times, it is hard to breathe, or even catch my breath. I have to breathe slowly and make my heart work in its proper function in order to regain the right breath. I love Him that much. For years, I had begged for the love I never had. I found it not in family, friends, a woman, or in anything else. However, when God and the Holy Spirit came, I knew at that very moment that no one could ever love me this much. To live with out His love, I surely would no longer wish to stay alive. His love cannot be matched nor put into words.

Please give all of my love to the Reverend Lew. I miss him very much. In addition, please share this letter with my friend Lew. I know he enjoys my letters and that to me personally is pure joy. I want only for him to be joyful and graced by our Father's love.

I will pray that I may be able to see all of you again soon. I hope that it is very soon indeed.

"We love you, but we could never love you as much as He does."

Brother Bob, Sister Ruth

"A Lonely Road" or "A New Beginning"

Aloha family, friends and all of God's children,

It's Christmas today.

I picked up one of my brothers, his wife, and her mother at the airport. I then took them, along with a ham and all the trimmings, to my niece's house for Christmas dinner. All of the other relatives will be there, but I have decided to spend my day alone with the Lord. Ruth, my wife, is spending her time at Waikiki with her brother and his family who are here visiting from Minnesota. I know everyone will have a delightful time. God bless all of them.

As I was sitting here channel surfing on the tube, I could not help but see so much evil and hurt in this world on most channels. There were the Christian channels, as well, but the majority featured people who were hurting over some tragic thing in their lives.

I began to reflect on my own life. How things have changed so wonderfully in it. It was a new life, a new beginning. I thought about the road that I was once on, with all of its sadness and shame, the loneliness and the tears, and of being on a road that just would never end. The more I tried to reach the end of that road, to find what was there, the more depressed I became.

I saw people being beaten, and others stealing and causing extreme pain to the heart. I saw knife fights, gunfights, and rape to not only others, but to myself as well. I saw dead bodies and men with missing limbs. I saw grown men cry like children over the loss of a friend. I saw the tears and felt the pain of my Mother's body as my father beat her. I cried myself to sleep night after night as a child, because I could not do anything to protect my family from a father, who found more comfort in a bottle of booze than he could find in his children's love for him. I hurt women emotionally because I could not commit to the love that was given to me. I did not know what love was, so I didn't know how to give it. What was "true" love?

Thinking about such things from the past would have caused me to do as my father did when he could not cope with life: grab a bottle of booze. That is exactly what I did for forty-five years, in fact. I became what my father was: an alcoholic. I had traveled the road of endless pain that each alcoholic travels. It is one of — if not the — loneliest roads one can take. I have tried to figure out why I went on that road, many, many times, and the one thing that keeps coming back in my mind is the lack of love from my father as a child.

One would think that as one grows older, he or she gets over the pain of childhood. I did not, I suppose. I was degraded as a child; I had no self-esteem, nor guidance from a teacher or uncle to pull me out of it. I learned at a young age that I was on my own. Therefore, I did what any growing child would do, with little or no knowledge of life: I rebelled. I tried to be as nice as possible but when I came home from Vietnam, I had no feeling left for compassion, nor did I want to find out what love was. I just did not care about anything anymore. Therefore, I would hide in a bottle. Drugs came and went. "Make-believe" love is all that I knew. I would watch out for myself, because no one else would. It was hard when I longed for love and compassion. It was very depressing and my best friend — the bottle — was not helping me at all.

One day, I decided to try again, after going through five treatment centers and countless veterans' hospitals. Four of my six brothers came down to California to get me off the streets. They "kidnapped" me, you could say. They took me to Seattle, and from there, I went to Hawaii with one of them. I was trying to help the homeless by myself. I was trying to stay sober.

It was not working. There were many things going on in my life and it was quite hard to stay focused. One day, I was tired of trying to do things by myself, so I decided to ask someone for help. All my life, I had done things my way, for the most part. However, I had hit bottom. I could not help anyone, with out help. I was very, very sad for the homeless, and I did not know anyone who would help me to help them. Therefore, I went to the only source I knew, the one who never gave up on me: I went to God.

I was not a religious person, nor what I thought a "religious" person was anyway. I got down on my knees and I began to cry for His help. I wanted Him to help me help those who could not help themselves. I knew the pain they felt. I had in my heart an overwhelming desire to help them, the way I knew they would be helped, with love. That is all they wanted in life, just as we all do. I begged God to help me to help them. From the heart, I asked. I asked Him to forgive me for all of the terrible things I did in my life. I was asking God to forgive me for things for which I could not forgive myself. I cried with a fearsome heart and only one who has prayed in such a way could understand it (besides God). God heard my heart, not my begging. He heard the sorrow in my heart and He knew that I was sincere.

What happened after that prayer, I would tell many. I know this to be true because He said it. He gave me a new road to travel, one that I know in my heart I shall never stray off. It is the road to Heaven and I am overwhelmed with each passing day. It is filled with all of the love that I had been searching for, for forty-five years. It is the most glorious feeling in this world, as we know it. One day, I pray I can come even a little closer to explaining just what "true love" is to a non-Christian.

So what am I grateful for this day? The birth of our Lord and Savior. How could I possibly be more grateful than to know Jesus Christ as my personal Savior? Just think about it: He gave His life for me. Not just for me, but for you, as well. Think about that. It seems to me that I was a fool and it may not have been my fault. However, I am sure of one thing: I have His overwhelming love and I want it no other way.

Please, please, ask Him — if you have not already — to forgive you for your sins so you too can feel the kind of love that only He can give to you. You will never be the same, and you will not want to be the way you were ever again.

God bless you. If ever you hear that knock at the door, open it up and invite Him in. He loves you so very much. Which do you prefer: a lonely road or a new beginning?

"I love you, but I could never love you as much as He does."

Brother Bob

Songs of the Children

Aloha, family, friends and all of God's children,

It is important that you know the reason I have had these letters published. The Lord wants to help all He can who are seeking wisdom. That is not to say that I am wise, but rather, grateful. Had it not been by the grace of God and His wisdom, I would not have been able to have these letters published at all.

For each Songs of the Children book that you buy, our 501(c) 3 organization will use the proceeds to purchase one of these books for a homeless person. Each donation in this endeavor goes to, "Songs of the Children". (Receipts sent, to those who wish, who donate.) This nonprofit company will then have the opportunity to not only give out a copy to many, but also be able to "give a hand up, not a hand out".

Please tell your family, friends, and all those who cross your path how they can help by buying one of these books.(Purchase at, "author-house. com") One thing that the homeless will do, just as everyone else, is that they will listen to someone "who has been there."

As you have read in a few of these letters, I have no desire for myself. I only wish to do as God tells me. I am blessed and you will be as well when you help those who need your helping hand.

Thank you for reading these letters and allowing me to share with you. I am sure that, by the grace of God, we will be able to help many. God Bless You. In addition, please remember,

"I love you, but I could never love you as much as He does."

Brother Bob

1 Peter 3:10 & 11

He who would love life
And see good days
Let him refrain his tongue from evil,
And his lips from speaking deceit.
Let him turn away from evil and do good.
Let him seek peace and pursue it.

Songs of the Children
P.O. BOX 8967
Honolulu, Hawaii 96830-0967
dunham@hawaii.rr.com

Everyday Hero Award

Shari Jay, Event Chair
American Red Cross Hawaii State Chapter

January 27, 2001

Robert Dunham, Director
Hosanna's House
PO Box 4376
Kailua-Kona, HI 96745

Dear Robert,

CONGRATULATIONS!

You have been nominated as an EVERYDAY HERO FOR 2000 for providing transitional shelter for homeless women in Kona. The American Red Cross - West Hawaii Branch wishes to recognize your achievements and present you with an award certificate at The Second Annual Everyday Heroes Breakfast at the Outrigger Waikoloa Beach Resort, Alii Ballroom, on Saturday, February 10, 2001, at 8:30 AM. There will be a photo session following the ceremonies at 11:30 AM.

As a Hero, you will be the guest of the American Red Cross to receive your award. Additional family members and friends are welcome to attend the event and may make reservations by calling the branch office at 326-9488 or Shari at 334-1569. Adults are $20 and children, 12 & under, are $10. Checks for additional guests may be made payable to: American Red Cross, and sent to the branch office at 74-5615 Luhia St. #A-1B, Kailua-Kona, HI 96740, (Attn: Heroes Breakfast)

We will be honoring nominees and winners in 14 categories including:

Good Samaritan Youth, Adult & Senior; Care Giver; Life Saver; Educator; Youth Educator; Animal Friend; Friend of the Ocean Environment; Friend of the Land Environment; Business; Organization; Youth Organization; and Life Time Achievement.

Please R.S.V.P. to either of the above numbers no later than February 5th. We look forward to seeing you on February 10th so you may be properly shown the appreciation of the American Red Cross for your humanitarian & heroic contributions to our community.

With Aloha,

Shari Jay, Event Chair
United Way Agency

Note: I show this award to you to show you how God has blessed His children thru me. It is in no way to give myself credit; it is to left up the Lord alone.

Brother Bob

A Vision

God's Ministry proudly presents:

Songs of the Children
(For All of God's Children)

I waited patiently for the Lord, and He inclined to me, and heard my cry. He also brought me up out of a horrible pit, out of the miry clay. He set my feet upon a rock and established my steps. "He has put a new song in my mouth"—Praise to our God. Many will see it and fear, and will trust in the Lord.

Ps 40:3

Brother Bob would like to introduce to you a singing group of God's children. They will delight your heart and soul, lift your spirits, raise your hopes, and guide you on your path in the Lord. Enjoy the oldies to the current hits and hear what the Lord has for you.

Come in, sit back, stand up, or jump up and down. The Lord has put new words into old songs that will cause the young, the old, the veteran, and the homeless to rise to the occasion.

"Praise be to God"

SONGS OF THE CHILDREN PRESENTS

"Gongs for the Songs"

FOR

HOSANNA'S HOUSE, A WOMAN'S SHELTER,
HALE KAINANA, A VETERAN'S HOMELESS SHELTER,
AND "SONGS OF THE CHILDREN," A CHRISTIAN
OUTREACH PROGRAM.

KEAUHOU SHOPPING CENTER SEPT. 23, 2000
8:15 AM – 9:00 AM AND AGAIN AT 10:00 AM – 10:45 AM
(SIX DIFFERENT ACTS PER SHOW)

PLEASE CONTACT BOB AT 326-1038 TO LET HIM
KNOW THAT YOU HAVE AN ACT FOR THE SHOW.
DEADLINE: FRIDAY, SEPTEMBER 15, 2000.
INFORMATIONAL MEETING FOR ALL TALENT AND
GONG ACTS AT KONA WEST CONDOS 6:00 PM
SEPTEMBER 16, 2000 (POT LUCK)

PRIZES INCLUDE: -- CAPTAIN BEANS –FAIRWIND –
KING KAM LUAU – BODY GLOVE – AND OTHER GIFTS
AS WELL, CALL NOW AND LET'S HAVE SOME FUN!

HOSTED BY: BROTHER BOB AND K-BIG RADIO

Made in the USA
San Bernardino, CA
17 November 2012